My Dancing Queen

CW00421530

Pe

INTRODUCTION

This book is dedicated to my late wife whom I loved, adored and worshiped. I will do forever, until eternity.

She left her ailing body behind on earth, a vessel which carried her real soul to join her past relatives in their eternal and spiritual environment.

She was born in 1941 and passed on Christmas Day 2018, at 12.06 am, painlessly. Her infectious and peaceful smile appeared on her face, which was by then free from pain and ageing.

She welcomed the end with defiance and by doing so she took away from death it's sting and glory by remembering at the last moment her grandmother's famous wise words:

"Only the wicked fear dying and if you live a respected life, after you pass, you will be missed for a long time and regretted by many."

IMPORTANT

Contents within this biography and symptoms apply only to Jill. If you are in any doubts, please always check it out with your GP. Early diagnosis saves life.

CHAPTER 1

My dancing queen was only seventeen when we first met in 1958. It was just before I was demobbed from the RAF after serving two years National Service, plus a third because I enjoyed the life. It was also a period of mass unemployment in the UK due to a crippling recession.

At the age of 21 I had already had my share of fun and girls galore. Also, I lived life to its full and never felt like settling down because I was, or thought I was, madly in love with an ex-school girlfriend until I found out that she was dating one of my best mates behind my back whilst I was away. That left me with mistrust, yet I wasn't much better than her, because I was also playing the field and got my just reward and deserved it.

Before my call up, and since the age of 10, I grew up with four good mates. We were more like brothers than friends and we spent most of our time together.

Being the same age, we were all called up to serve in the armed forces. I chose the RAF, another chose the Royal Navy, the third the Army. However, our fourth friend, who stole my girlfriend, failed on medical grounds "hereditary flat feet" and decided to bluff his way into the Merchant Navy.

Although the gang was broken up, we still made arrangements to meet up on our 48 hours leave and carried on with the best time of our lives, as we knew it then.

One weekend only my friend Micky and I managed to meet up. His father and mother were away, and they left their Baby Austin 7 car behind. We decided to borrow it as he had a licence and mine was only to ride a motor bike.

We made two checks, one was to make sure that we replaced the petrol we would use as it was rationed in those days, also so that his father wouldn't notice that we borrowed his car. The other was to work out how much money we had left over from our £2.10 shillings weekly wage, which is now equal to £2.50, mind you in comparison with this day and age it went a long way.

On our way back from the petrol station, after topping the car up with half a gallon, we saw two girls walking along the pavement eating chips from a newspaper, that was also the way they wrapped fish and chips in those so called "good old days".

Micky asked me to stop them and use my charms and chat them up. He immediately took a fancy to the taller one of the two, so I told him that she would tower over him as he was shorter than her.
 He replied.
  "This is my dad's car, so I choose first"
I wasn't very happy with his reply and said.
  "Very childish, but what does one expect from the Army?"
He burst out laughing and replied.
  "Respect Brylcream boy" … "Respect"
I agreed and asked him to pull over, by the way that was also the norm in those days to speak to girls out of a car's window.

I spoke to the shorter of the two girls and said.
  "Can you spare a couple of chips for a hungry airman and a starving down in the ranks common soldier please Miss?"
Micky wasn't impressed with my approach and whispered one word back to me.
  "Bastard!"

The young girl, who was heavily made up, replied.
  "Get your own bleedin' chips" … "Besides if you two can afford a car, then you can also afford to buy your own fish as well as chips. You can treat us as well whilst you are about it!"

Both girls blanked us out and carried on walking. They kept turning around sticking their tongues out at us and laughing. Both my ego and reputation were at stake and I felt deflated, but I wasn't going to let them off that easily, so I said to Micky.

"Go on, catch up with them and pull up again."

So, I tried a different approach and this time spoke to the taller one and said.

"You are more beautiful than your shorter friend, maybe the fresh air up there is clean and doing you a world of good" … "Give us a chip please?" … "Tell you what, we'll do a deal with you, as there is a bus-strike on we will only give you a lift and not your tight-fisted mean friend, she can walk home on her own."

With an angry and raised voice, replied.

"You heard my mate, just do yourselves a big favour now and piss off before I report you to the Old Bill for harassment."

The shorter one quickly stopped us from moving off, she rummaged through her chips, picking out the smallest, and by the look on her face which was unmistakable she didn't really want to part with it, and said.

"Although your approach is a bit corny mate, and it's gone past its sell by date, your smile is lovelier. Here, share this one between you and don't ask for any more cos you ain't going to get any."

Amazing as it may sound, and during that split moment in time, I fell head over heels and madly in love with her, don't ask me why, I just did. I had a strong urge to get out of the car and kiss her and not for the chip.

So, I replied after taking a bite from the tiny chip, and passed the rest to my friend.

"That tasted just like Ambrosia darling."

She looked mystified, then began to laugh and replied.

"That was only a bleedin' chip you nut case."

Opportunity knocked and I said.

"How about a date sweetheart?"

She replied.

"Let me have a look in my diary first, to see if I can fit you in?"

Then she began to laugh and looked down at the empty palm of her hand and pretended to read, then said.

"You're in luck, nothing" … "Besides why do you want to date us?"

I answered.

"My friend and I are very lonely and on a short leave from the forces, also we are returning to our camps tomorrow. I promise that by the time the date is over you will fall madly in love with me" … "Let's not waste any more time in our lives" … "Tell me, where do you live gorgeous so that I can pick you up?"

She pointed and replied.

"Across the road, and down those steps to the right."

"Well I never!" … "I live further down to the left, where the pub is" … "We are neighbours"

"Just a sec. I will ask me mate first to see if she wants to come, otherwise I am not allowed to go out alone with you or any other boy because my dad will kill me."

The two girls began to whisper, and the shorter one returned and said.

"Right there will be conditions and if you agree to all we will go on a date, consider yourself privileged"

She smiled, looked at her friend and winked, then carried on saying.

"You pay" … "No touching or kissing" … "We also want to go to the pictures to see Ginger the Millionaire Cat."

I stopped her and said.

"I hate bleedin' cats"

She calmly replied.

"That's your hard luck, we love them" …. "Please let me finish" …. "Right, like it or not you will have to partner me and not my friend, cos she doesn't like you" … "Last conditions, we all walk, no cars and back seat snogging, and we decide when we want to go home" … "Also, we will tell you if we want to see you again."

"Tall order Miss, what time shall we pick you up and what's your house number?"

"Dead on six and here."

"What are your names?"

"Mine is Jill with a "J" and my mate is Val"

I laughed and said.

"With a "V", I presume."

"Ha. Ha. Ha, I don't think that was very funny" …   "What are your names?" … "Don't tell me, let me guess, "Bill and Ben" the flower pot men."

I laughed and replied

"So, you think that was funny?"

"Yeah"

"Mine is Peter, and my mate's is Micky."

She began to laugh and replied.

"With a "P" I presume?"

I replied.

"Touché"

"WOOW! Showing off your bit of French as well I see."

They left and crossed the road and we carried on to my house. When we got there, we found that we only had £2 between us. I said to Mick.

"Can you get your hands on extra cash?"

"Not legally! Tell you what we'll do, we got another three hours before we meet up with those tarts"

I stopped him in his tracks and told him to withdraw the word tarts, he began to laugh and changed it to lovely tarts then carried on saying.

"Where was I, oh yeah, we'll stick a bit of cardboard in the "B" button section of the public phone box which is round the corner, then go to the Off Licence opposite and I will climb over the wall, by the way we will need a blanket because there is barbed wire on it, we will nick a few returns and I will pass them on to you and sell them back to the bloke. You will have to go in because I've already been caught once, and he'll remember me face."

"I am so desperate to see Jill again I would even go as far as to rob a bank" … "You know Mick I bet you anything in the world, also mark my word today and read my lips carefully, I am going to marry her"

"You're daft Pete, you don't even know her" … "I recon the Air Force have brain washed you mate"

We followed Mick's plan and managed to raise another £1.12 shillings.

CHAPTER 2

The next three hours went so slow and we turned up at the arranged meeting spot ten minutes early. When the girls arrived the four of us walked to the cinema with little conversation.

During the interval Mick asked the girls if they would like a "choc-ice" and both agreed, they asked for a cold drink as well.

I whispered in Mick's ear.

"Alright big mouth, now tell me, where are you going to get the money from?"

"Never thought of that Pete."

Jill was sitting next to me and began to tap my hand, I thought great she is coming on to me, but instead she placed a ten shillings note in the palm of my hand and whispered.

"It's only a loan and I want it back"

Every time our arms touched during the film, we both quickly distanced ourselves, it was mental torture because all I wanted to do was to get closer to her and only put my arm around her. She was also drawing me closer with her vibes just like a magnet would draw a piece of metal, but I kept losing my nerve and that had never happened to me before. That was when I found out she was different from any other girl I had ever met before.

On our way back Mick and Val walked in front whilst Jill and I behind in conversation.

She asked me.

"Do you fly planes?"

"No, I am in the legal department, but do a lot of flying" ….

"By the way, I am getting demobbed in six months' time."

"What will you do after?"

"I honestly don't know." … "I may join the Merchant Navy to see more of the world"

She replied with all the confidence in the world.

"My dad works in the Print and if we are still an item, I will ask him to get you a job" … "It's a closed shop mind you, but it's who you know."

I asked her.

"What about you?"

"I just finished my course in needle work at college and got an apprenticeship with a posh firm in the West End, they make dresses for the Royals and film stars."

"Wow! That's very impressive Jill"

"I wish you didn't have to go back tomorrow, I sort of got to like you."

That sounded like sweet music to my ears.

I replied.

"I am madly in love with you and I want to marry you, after that I want to get to know more about you"

She began to laugh, and drew Val and Mick's attention, and then she said to me.

"Now you're taking the piss big time."

I replied with an American accent and said.

"You just wait and see blue eyes."

You know she had the most beautiful, sparkling and smiling azure eyes, yet they had a tinge of sadness about them as if she was hiding deep sorrow and heart ache.

We arrived outside her house, she shook my hand and rushed to her front door, then turned round and said.

"Will you come round before you go back; please say that you will?"

"I can't, I have to be on parade by eight thirty in the morning and will be leaving early, I will write to you though"

"That will be nice, I will look forward to your letters, hope you can write? If not get one of your mates to write it for you"

I laughed and replied.

"Cheeky monkey."

Then I threw her a kiss.

In the meantime, Mick left to see Val home.

When I got back to my house, I knocked on the door because I left my keys behind, my mother opened the door for me and said.

"What was she like?"

Thinking that she saw us I replied.

"How did you know I was out with a girl?"

"Your face says it all and your shirt has got make up on it"

"I don't know how the makeup got on it because we only shook hands" …. "Tell you what mum, I am in love and found my future wife; she lives just round the corner and she is also the most beautiful girl in the world, besides you that is."

"Stop that silly talk, I've made a couple of sandwiches, one is for Joe. He left a loaf behind and said he will pick you up at half past five in the morning; and you are be ready because you made him late last time"

"I may go absent without leave because I just don't want to leave Jill behind"

"I see you've been drinking again, besides why don't you ask her to join the Airforce then you will be able to see her every day"

She began to laugh and went up to her bedroom.

Joe by the way was one of our neighbours and also by sheer coincidence he worked for the Wonder loaf bakery and delivers bread to our camp, he often gave me a lift back in his van when I didn't have my motor bike with me.

I returned to the camp and felt extremely melancholy because all I wanted was to see Jill again.

CHAPTER 3

Jill and I exchanged several letters over the next two weeks. In her last one she asked if I didn't mind going out alone with her because Val and Mick couldn't get on, they kept arguing and they had gone their separate ways. She said not to worry too much about it though because her dad had given his permission, only because she kept nagging him and bribed him with an extra portion of his favourite oxtail stew.

The long and awaited leave, which felt as if a lifetime, finally arrived. I had decided to take a week off from my annual leave, I had written to Jill and asked her to do the same, if she could that is. She replied and told me that she was unable to because she didn't have any time due but said that she would report sick though.

I arrived home, had a quick bath, and then afterwards showered in Old Spice aftershave that I used to get free from an American airman friend of mine who was stationed with me at West Drayton.

My mother knocked on my bedroom door and gave me a clean ironed shirt. I thanked her, then rewarded her with a kiss on the cheek and said.
 "I just don't know what I'll do without you mum"
She smiled back and said.
 "Don't get any makeup on it and I only hope your new girlfriend can iron, cook, wash your dirty socks and pants for you."
 "Don't you worry about that mum, I will bring her back here so that you and my three sisters can teach her, but somehow I think she is already house trained because she likes cats."

I was out of my house like a bolt of lightning and headed to our local florist first on my way. The lady there was one of my ex's and recommended red and white roses on the house for old times' sake and hoped that there will not be any more bad feelings between us.

She then asked me who the lucky girl was, and I tried to describe Jill to her.

"You don't deserve any one like her, she went to my school, a very nice girl and I hope you don't mess her about like you did me, the poor girl has enough on her plate to cope with right now without you adding any more to her problems."

"Like what?"

"You obviously don't know; she will tell you in her own time"

"I hope she's not a bloke in disguise?"

She burst out laughing and replied.

"Stay as you are and never change" … "You are still as mad as a bloody hatter."

I left the shop and headed towards Jill's house.

The closer I got the faster my heart began to beat, my mouth dried up and I even seemed to have forgotten what Jill looked like.

I found the house, number 28 and knocked on the door. I noticed that her front room curtains moved and then she came to the door and opened it. She smiled and gave me a kiss on the cheek.

We walked to her kitchen, come dining room, and a middle-aged man greeted me with a smile and spoke with a cockney east end London accent, not only did he look but amazingly sounded just like Arthur Mallard a T.V. actor. We shook hands and he said.

"So, at long last, you're Pe'er. Thank God you've turned up cos she's been driving us all round the bleedin' bend since she got to know ya" … "Do you fancy a cuppa?" … "By the way me name is Harry, we know what your bleedin' name is, so do all of our neighbours."

"Thanks Harry I could murder one."

I had my very welcomed cup of tea, mind you I fancied something stronger than tea.

Jill took hold of my hand and led me upstairs.
On our way up she said.
   "Don't get too ambitious, I am only going to introduce you to my lovely nan, she just can't wait to see you"
I laughed and replied.
   "Shame, I thought my luck has changed"
   "Remember, no touching, well at least not yet."

We entered the room upstairs and there was a lovely matured lady sitting by the window.
Jill introduced us. Her name was Louise and I fell madly in love with her because I missed out on my own grandmothers.
After a short while we left and returned to the downstairs room. On entering I noticed a young girl about 12 years old who was a little on the tubby side and a young man about two years older than me. Jill introduced us, it was her younger sister Jennifer, and her older brother David.

She then suggested we take a walk in the Local Park, but we will not be alone. On our way we knock on her cousin's house first because Jill promised to take her newly born baby out in her pram. I was introduced to her cousin and we carried on to the park.

We sat on a bench and talked. I asked her.
   "Excuse me Jill, I know it's none of my business, but where is your mother?"
She burst out crying.
I sat and thought... "What have I done; maybe I should have waited till she told me?"
   "I am very sorry Peter, it's no fault of yours, she is in Groveland's Home recovering after having her breast removed, she has cancer"
   "Oh, No!" ... "I am so sorry to hear that."
With a positive tone in her voice she answered.

"She, "WILL" get better"

"Can we go to visit her?"

"That's nice, do you mean yo

"Not at all, because you an

ahead of us, especially when wε

of our families and friends.

"Thank you, she will love that."

I then asked her.

"Do you have a boyfriend?"

"Did have"

"What went wrong?"

"He was only after one thing and thε ͟ ͟ ͟ ϲo get his leg over my precious body; mind you, neither he nor anybody else have had their wicked way with me yet, and also it's not on the menu. I will decide when after making sure that he's the right man, besides that he kept moaning and groaning all the bleeding time about me spending too much time looking after my family whilst my mum is sick" ... "You know what Peter?"

She stopped short then bit on her bottom lip, at the same time her face turned bright red."

I smiled and said.

"Go on, don't be shy carry on"

"I think you're a smashing bloke compared with him"

"You are absolutely right Jill, and I can assure you that your taste in men has now improved considerably."

She answered.

"Big head"

We both burst out laughing and woke the baby up.

We left the park, dropped the baby back to her cousin, and then carried on to her house. We decided that in the afternoon we would go and visit her mother, but before that I had to be honest with her and said.

"The car you saw us in wasn't ours"

She stopped me and said with a shocked face.

"I hope you didn't nick it?"

I laughed and replied.

, it belonged to Mick's dad" …

…d went to my wallet, then took out one
…e and handed it to her and carried on saying.
,ou will let me off the interest and don't charge
…y?"
…e laughed and replied.

"I forgot about that, thanks" … "That proves one thing to me that you're not a ponce"

"By the way Jill, do you like motor bikes?"

"I love them, but my dad won't allow me to ride on one or go anywhere near them."

"Oops!" … "I only own an old BSA Bantam, ex Post Office bike, and it cost me £5 in an auction, it was as cheap as chips."
She replied.

"You are not still having a pop at me about that chip. Take this 10 Bob back, it will pay for the bus tickets when we go to see my mum"

"Thank you but I do have some money also being in forces, I travel free."
She gave me a gentle kiss on the cheek, smiled and we then parted company.

I felt more nervous on my return to her and stopped at the florist and asked her what she would recommend this time; and told her that I now know all about Jill's problem with her mother.
She replied and said.

"She is one lovely lady and never failed to invite me and Jill's other friends in when we knocked on her" … "Right let's get back to business; start digging deep this time because it's not on the house" … "Two bunches of roses and two boxes of Belgium chocolates; diplomacy goes a long way darling Peter and try not to be the last of the big spenders."

I knocked on Jill's door and she answered it.
Her eyes nearly popped out of their sockets and said.

"They are lovely and so are you too, I just love creeps, mum will love them and you too. Thanks Peter."

We walked to the High Road and got on a number 29 bus to Southgate which was only a short walk from where her mother's rehabilitation home was. When we got there and entered the ward her mother saw us and beckoned us over with a smile.

Jill then introduced me to her. Her name was Rose. I passed the roses first and said.
  "A rose for a lovely Rose and you're more beautiful than these roses."
She did exactly as Jill did when I embarrassed her, although Rose's face was pale and drain from colour because of her sickness but it still turned slightly red, and she bit on her bottom lip.

I looked at Jill and noticed that she was standing with tears pouring down her cheeks and she then said to her mother.
  "He's a right creep and a charmer mum, but there's no harm in him" … "He likes the older woman and loves to show off."
Jill then suggested that we took her mother out in a wheel chair for a bit of fresh air in the grounds and I was to push her because she did her share of pushing prams in the morning.

We went to see the sights in London and had a bite to eat after a trip on the River. We then returned home on the underground feeling exhausted.

After that visit our relationship was almost cemented, we became very good friends and just short of being an item.

The gang broke up simply because they kept telling me that Jill was not good enough for me and I should ditch her. One weekend the four of us met in our local pub and an argument broke out between us after they gave me an ultimatum, that was to either choose Jill or them. It didn't take me long to arrive to an irrevocable decision and told the so-called friends to get stuffed and then walked away feeling almost bereaved and broken hearted.

I went to Jill's house and knocked on her door, it was late, she opened it and with a shocked look on her face when she saw me looking sad, also wondered why I was calling on her at a late hour because I was supposed to be out with my mates. I told her what had happened, and she invited me in.

I noticed that she was knitting a Navy-Blue woollen men's jumper and asked her.
   "Who's the lucky man?"
She replied.
   "I never tell lies, it started as a surprise present to Stan, my ex, but after ditching him it will be yours now if you are still around and don't walk out on me before I finish knitting it."
   "But you've got one sleeve longer than the other Jill."
She held it up and began to laugh, and I joined her; by doing so I realised that I made the right choice with my decision earlier with my ex-friends.
She then said.
   "Oh! I never noticed that, besides he was a lot shorter than you"
   "I think you and I should get married quick, just in case you find someone else shorter than me again"
   "Is this a proposal? If so, you will have to go down on one knee; don't worry too much I will help you up again, I know you're getting on a bit"
I went down on one knee as ordered and said.
   "You WILL marry me, like it or not. Also, I will not take NO for an answer."
   "You sounded just like a chauvinist pig just now, course I will, BUT... you will have to ask me mum and dad first and have to wait till I am eighteen"
I replied.
   "So, we are now provisionally engaged?"

As soon as I stood up, we kissed for the very first time, let me emphasize on that, I meant we really kissed because she felt soft, warm, and heavenly in my arms as if we were floating on a cloud, or a magic carpet.

I took a whiff and said.
  "You smell heavenly, what perfume do you wear?"
She blushed and replied.
  "I just had a bath, it's Johnson's baby powder."

I decided to go home early because she was returning to work; we walked together to her door and stood on her porch then carried on kissing. Neither of us wanted to stop, until her father pulled up in his car after arriving from his night shift. He asked me if I was coming or going; I replied that I was going. He said.
  "Good night son, nice to see you again"
I replied.
  "Good night Harry"
I left and went home.

As soon as I entered, I saw my parents relaxing and listening to the radio. Very soon after I entered the room they were no longer relaxed especially when I burst out with excitement and told them that I just got engaged. My mother immediately, stood up and turned the gas light on the wall brighter, we used to use it to subsidise the electric bill, she then said.
  "You are drunk again, one day you will get yourself in trouble, I hope you didn't have any witnesses because breach of promise is very expensive nowadays."

They both sat in a state of shock and stared at me as if I had just committed a crime. My mother broke the silence and said.
  "We don't even know what she looks like; you haven't got a job to go to when you get demobbed; where are you going to get money from to live on?"

I stopped her in her tracks and angrily replied.

"I am going to marry Jill and live with her, and not with you mum; besides when her father gets to know that I am serious, and also approves of me with her mother, he will get me work in the print; all I need right now is your blessings and not a bloody lecture mum."

I agreed with her that after her parents knew, also at the same time hoped that they approved, I would bring Jill home to meet them. I expected my father to object more than my mother, but he just kept quiet, shook his head and returned his attention to his music.

The next morning after a sleepless night, only because all of a sudden reality hit me hard, I got out of bed and had a quick wash then rushed to Jill's house. She opened the door, smiled and said.

"I hope you haven't changed your mind and it wasn't the booze talking last night?"

"No, my angel, I just missed you" … "Have you said anything to your father yet?"

"No, I waited till you come round. I also got the second greatest news this morning, the first you already know about, and that was last night; my dad just told me that mum is coming out today; I reckon it's best to wait till they are both here to ask them; what do you think?"

"Perfect but will the shock affect your mother's health?"

"No, I know my mum well, she will approve of you, but don't you dare spoil her with roses and chocolates; just be warned, my dad gets very jealous quick, also he is an ex-boxing champ of Islington."

"Thanks for the warning"
Jill then asked me.

"Tell me please; when will I meet your parents?"

"When your dad approves, and if I am still in one piece that is; mind you could always be introduced to them at my funeral"

"You know Peter you are my lucky charm and my hero; you have turned my whole life around to the best"

"Thank you, Jill with a " J"."

CHAPTER 4

Jill asked me if I wanted to go with them to pick her mother up, I declined because I thought it was an occasion for the immediate family to be alone and told her that I will come around later.

Rose was picked up, there were celebrations and jubilations in Jill's house and no room for outside intruders. She sent her sister to my house to ask why I wasn't there with them, and also told her not to return without me. Rather than to disappoint her I decided to leave with Jennifer.

Jill greeted us at the door and asked me with a raised voice.
    "Where the hell have you been?"
I replied.
    "Sorry Jill, I thought it was the time for the immediate family to be together"
    "You are family now you silly sod"
    "Thank you, I also consider that as an honourable compliment."
    "Give us a quick kiss before my cousins grab hold of you; by the way even mum asked where you were you must have left a good impression on her."
I thought this is just getting better.
Jennifer tutted and said.
    "You will have to excuse me you two whilst I go to the loo and stick my finger down my throat."
Jill laughed and replied.
    "You're only jealous."
I suggested to Jill before I left and told her we will ask her parents tomorrow when the dust has settled; she said that she can't wait and agreed.

As soon as I got back home, my mother with a very serious look on her face said.
    "That was a child Peter; she can't be more than 12 years old and I also hope that you
haven't already been too familiar with her."

I began to laugh and replied.

"That was her younger sister silly mum"

Then I explained the situation with regards to her mother.
I was astonished by my mother's reaction when she told me to immediately return and
bring Jill back with me.

"I promise to do just that and will tomorrow; thank you, mother."

The next day and on entering Jill's house I saw her mother and father, with her brother, sister and nan all sittings joyously together. I was greeted with warm smiles from all which
made me feel guilty just in case my request to marry Jill went wrong.

She nudged me after engaging her hand in my arm and then whispered.

"Well what are you waiting for, ask?"

With an extremely nervous voice I said.

"Rose it's nice to see that you are back home where you belong"

She smiled and thanked me then replied.

"I wasn't born yesterday, I've just got a feeling you have something on your mind, go on be brave son and spit it out"

She then began to laugh.

"Thank you for making it easier for me; I won't beat about the bush; I know Jill and I have only just met and I love her very much" … "Also, I will be demobbed from the RAF very soon and want to look after her till death us do part." … "Please allow me to marry her?"

"Unusual approach and different, but she's only seventeen Peter; I know she has an old head on very young shoulders and that's only because of me; my sickness forced her into an adult's life; she hasn't had any time to enjoy her youth yet."

"So why should we waste any more time; life is very short Rose, and I will make sure that she will not miss out on anything."

"You seem to be a mature enough young man, and know that you will spoil her silly" … "It's okay by me but her father will have to give his consent as well."

Jill looked at her father and then begged him by saying.

"Please dad; I will still look after you all"

Harry's face turned as red as a ripe tomato and replied.

"Right it looks like you've made up your own minds and bed, now you will have to lay in it. Hold on don't get too bleedin' excited, after you get hitched that is"… "Jill also told me that you ain't got a job when you come out of the Air Force, so I'll get you a union card for the print, it will help you out, if it's alright with you that is?"

Jill's face quickly beamed with a smile, she left my side and gave her mother and then her father and nan a kiss.

Jennifer and David looked on bewildered and then both burst out laughing.

David said.

"Cor blimey Pete that took a lot of bottle"

Her mother with tears of joy removed a ring from her finger without any effort, because she had lost a lot of weight and passed it to me, then said.

"I don't have to ask you to look after her because I know you will; have a good life together and start now, because no one knows what's around the corner" … "Also, this ring has been handed down to me from my mother who is sitting over there with a smile of approval on her face" … "By the way Peter let me warn you she is a very crafty old woman, but you can always bribe her when the ice-cream van pulls up outside the house, she will start licking her lips"

"Thank you Rose, I will also make sure that I look after you as well as I would look after my own mother, father and three sisters not forgetting my older brother"

Rose smiled and said.

"Well what are you waiting for; kiss her you fool."

We kissed, and that became the best and most magical day in my life so far, also a day which I will never ever forget until my dying day.

We left Jill's house and headed to mine. On the way Jill engaged her hand proudly into my arm, I felt like the king of the road with my queen next to me. Passers-by who where our neighbours and knew us both, although Jill and I never crossed paths before, acknowledged us with smiles.

Jill squeezed my arm and said.

"Why all of a sudden I am shitting myself?"

She stopped and said.

"OOPS!" ... "I am so sorry that slipped out"

As soon as we arrived and waited for the door to open, I seemed to have developed Jill's ailment and said to her.

"When we get in you rush upstairs to the first door on the right and I will use the outside loo"

We both burst out laughing and she replied.

"SHOOSH! Please don't make me laugh, I will wet myself on this doorstep."

One of my sisters opened the door and she seemed to have known Jill and said.

"Whatcha Jill, come on in, also let me warn you we are all mad in this family"

When we entered the front room, my father was sitting in his armchair and reading his paper; he acknowledged Jill with a smile and returned to his paper.

There was a thunderous noise from the hall way as the rest of the family rushed down the stairs and entered the room with Prince our mixed breed dog wagging his tail and barking.

My mother finally came in from the kitchen.

Yes, it was my day of judgement and you might as well say Jill's too. She looked at Jill from head to toe and repeated her action several times which left the poor girl very nervous.

I said.

"This is Jill mum" ... "Jill meet my mother"

My mother smiled but not convincingly and said to Jill.

"Pleased to meet you at long last" ... "I didn't realise you were that short Jill"

I quickly intervened as I noticed Jill's face turn red and said.

"It's quality that counts more than quantity mother, besides she is the same height as you five foot odd; it is I who is tall"

My mother replied with a sarcastic tone in her voice and said.

"You may be more accurate on the odd but not the measurements."

One of my sisters noticed that Jill was very hurt and embarrassed and said.

"Don't take any notice of her Jill she is hormonal"

Mother soon changed her approach and went over to Jill and then cuddled and gave her a kiss on each cheek then said.

"Sorry Jill I was only joking just like my clown son does. You are very beautiful, and I am so pleased my son found you" … "Also, pleased and sure that you will be good for him, as I have always been" … "I am also pleased to hear that your mother is out of hospital and recovering from that dreadful disease. Please wish her well and tell her we are all ready to give her a helping hand if ever she needs us."

"Thank you; that's very nice of you to say so."

Looking very impressed my mother said.

"That's a very beautiful, and expensive ring; has my son robbed a bank?"

"Not yet, my mother passed it on to me, it's a very important family heirloom, priceless and to be honest with you no bank has enough money to buy it."

We left my mother's house and returned to Jill's home. As we were walking back, I noticed that Jill was not happy and asked her what was wrong. She told me that my mother didn't like her, but I corrected and convinced her that my mother had very funny and peculiar ways of expressing her affection because it's the way she and my father were both brought up by their parents who were strict Victorians, also in my own opinion I thought she adored her.

We made arrangements with our parents about the wedding. Due to shortage of funds we decided to have a small and simple white church wedding. The church we decided to marry at was Saint Marks in Noel Park, Wood Green, it was also the same church which I used to be a choir boy in.

CHAPTER 5

Demob day finally arrived as I crossed the last day off my calendar, I took it out of my locker threw it on the ground and danced up and down on it.

I arranged with Allan, an old school friend of mine, to come to my camp and help me bring back an old two-seater 1929 drop-head Morris sports car, a gift from an American Airman who was stationed with me at West Drayton.

Allan drove the car back home because I only had a provisional licence to drive a car. On our way the gear stick came away from its socket, being a motor mechanic Allan replaced the stick with a large screw driver, and we carried on our way after having a good laugh. I thanked Allan and bought him five cigarettes, he also promised to repair the car free of charge for me.

My kit bag was still in the back of the car, so I decided to call on Jill to show my car off to her.
She opened her front door and then rushed towards me, we kissed and embraced each other. She looked at the car and burst out laughing.
I was hurt and asked her.
 "Excuse me Jill, what's so funny?"
My brother knows a yard which will take that old banger and may also give you a couple of bob for it."
She carried on laughing and began to cross her legs saying.
 "Oh don't!" … "I am going to wet myself for sure this time"
 "Come on stop taking the piss, I will give you a drive round the block in it and I am sure you will take that remark back after you will see how nice it is."

She sat in the passenger seat and was still laughing out of control. I said to her.
"Come on it's not that bad. You can give the interior a clean-up and I will buy a tin of paint from the oil shop and change

the colour also to show you how much I love you I will even let you choose it."

We moved off and all of a sudden, she started to laugh again and this time she was almost hysterical and repeating her self several times by saying.

"Oh, don't"

I took my eyes off the road to see what was so funny and began to laugh with her as I noticed a plank of wood in her hand from the floor and she was looking through a gap onto the road.

When we got to the street which led to my house, after leaving a cloud of white smoke behind us, we turned left and drove towards my house to say hello to my parents. A police Sergeant on his bicycle waved me down. It was one of our neighbours, Sergeant Watkins.

He took his hat off and wiped the perspiration from his forehead then said.

"Hello! Hello! Hello!... What have we got here?"

I nervously answered.

"Just got demobbed Sergeant Watkins and I am showing my fiancé Jill how nice my car is"

With a loud voice he said.

"Out! Take your kit bag with you and get your brother to drive it home. I know you only have a provisional licence and I also notice that there is no Tax disc on the windscreen. Furthermore, I am 100% sure it's not insured?"

He carried on saying and at the same time he was trying to control his laughter.

"By the way my heartiest congratulations on your demob and engagement"

He then looked at Jill, smiled and carried on. "Hurry up and marry him, even my own daughter is madly in love with him and you've got a good man there" ... "Go on and behave yourself, I've also got my beady eyes on you young Peter"

I began to laugh and replied.

"I didn't know you cared Sergeant Watkins."

Jill burst out laughing after we walked away with my kit bag on my shoulder and said to me.

"You are one bloody criminal; a good man, I should say so?"

"May I suggest to really celebrate my freedom from the forces we buy fish and chips for all tonight round your house"

"Who pays?"

"Me of course, I am loaded, I got my demob pay and took cash instead of one of their three piece grey civvies street suits"

With concern on her face she said.

"We've got to be a little more careful from now on how we spend our money, because of the wedding"

"Have no fear, Pete the provider is here"

"You can be a right flashy git on the quiet"

The family arrived back home that evening, and Jill told them about my treat.

Her brother laughed and said.

"Top hat and tails? Or can we keep our working clothes on."

"Ex-army, I understand from Jill and also you were discharged because you conveniently developed skin problems from your uniform"

"My little sister has got a big mouth, but I still love the pair of ya"

She and I took their orders and walked to the local fish and chip shop.

I said to Jill.

"I hope I didn't upset your bother?"

"No, he loves you like he would love his own brother if he had one"

On our way back we stopped and kissed; afterwards we opened one of the portions of chips, I took out two chips, one very large and the other was the smallest I could find after rummaging through them and passed her the smallest. She thought back to the first time we met when she rummaged through her portion of chips and gave Mick and I the smallest.

She looked up at me and said.

"I am slowly but surely beginning to tumble you."

After we all had an extremely enjoyable meal, we remained seated at the table and began to discuss more plans for our wedding. Jill suggested that with help from her cousin, who was also handy with a needle, they could both make the wedding and the bridesmaids dresses as that would be a great saving. Also, we could buy readymade sandwiches and have the reception upstairs in our local pub and the landlord would give us a discount on the drinks if we buy them from him. Rose asked.

"Where are you planning to go for your honeymoon?"

I suggested a dirty night out at the Strand Palace hotel, and in time we will have a proper honeymoon, one which Jill will never forget.

From that day on, life began to be a dream come true. Jill and I in the short time of being single made sure that we lived the "Life of Riley" and stole every moment of happiness, by laughing, dancing, ice skating and partying.

I tried several times to get physical with her, but she continually turned me down and told me to wait as it wasn't that long now and used to laugh it off to ease my embarrassment and say.

"Just remember your mother waited nine months to have for you."

Harry kept his promise and got me a union card to work in the print, but because of the late night work I told him that I wasn't really cut out for that kind of work and I will try to get work in the City because I have a little knowledge about export and shipping which I
learned from my father. I also took a course in a London college which was paid for by the RAF and qualified with a degree.

Luck was on my side because after several failed attempts to get the work which I wanted I was offered a position with a tea company only because I was beginning to get desperate and walked into the building and asked the manager for work. Being an ex-service man, he admired my courage when I walked into his office without an appointed. After the very short interview he took a chance and offered me a junior position and started me with a wage of £10.50 a week. I knew that I could better myself in time.

Jill carried on working with the dressmaking company in the West End and we travelled daily by underground on the same line and I got off at Old Street station and she carried onto Green Park station.

We set our wedding day for the first week in October. We were offered temporary accommodation by both of our parents after we were married until we could stand up on our own two feet which was very much appreciated.

The stage was now set and the preparations for the wedding were going full steam ahead and according to plan, with one exception, time began to run slowly because Jill and I couldn't wait for our happy day.

CHAPTER 6

It finally arrived, the 3rd of October 1959, our wedding day. *You know as I am writing this there are tears filling my eyes and the page has gone hazy (by the way it takes true love and a real man to cry).*

In Jill's house, her cousin and mother made sure that she looked like a princess and both were closely supervised by her nan and sister; mind you Jill didn't need much work on her because nature already had blessed her with beauty.

In my house, my mother and sisters were adjusting my suit, hair and tie, whilst my friend Allan with help from my brother were both pulling faces and ridiculing me.

I decided to walk to the church with Allan and my brother who was the best man, I had turned down a lift offered by one of my father's friends who owned my dream car, a white Jaguar.

Allan asked me how I felt and told him like a bloody chicken going to have a close shave. He began to laugh and said that he equally felt the same because Linda his finance will be there and bound to start nagging him into the same chicken parlour. My brother stepped in and said that he has already taken that walk and heard that the first fifty years are the worst, but it does get better especially when your hearing starts to fail and only see their mouth move up and down. We passed several of friends and they said.
  "Good luck Pete, you will need it mate."

We arrived to the slaughter house, sorry I meant the church, there were so many people there which included neighbours from both sides who wished us well. My biggest surprise of all was when I noticed my old three friends there.

We entered the church after greeting some and I shook hands with the three and told them they were welcome to the reception, also thanked them for being there and making it a perfect day so far for me.

My brother and I sat in the front row and waited for Jill's arrival. It seemed ages, and I kept telling my brother to go out and see if everything was alright, he calmly said to me.

"For God's sake Peter, just relax man, they all make you sweat on purpose" ... "Besides the longer you wait the better it will taste."

The organ began to play the wedding march, the priest told everybody to stand but I was frozen in my seat and could not move until my brother helped me up and said.

"You do know that you have to go and stand in front of him at the altar, I just can't see him bringing Jill over to you" I asked him.

"What does she look like?" and he replied.

"I will swap her for mine any day; absolutely stunning and worth the wait."

I could smell and feel her closeness as she arrived and stood next to me. It was just like a magical sweet dream. She was stunning alright, and the description did not do her any justice, there wasn't any other word written to describe the way she looked at that moment in time. I could see her sparkling blue eyes smiling through her veil as the light of the altar candles flickered and added the element of mystique to them.

The ceremony began and after Harry placed her shaking hand into mine, he wiped his tears with his handkerchief then returned and stood next to Rose.

After the ceremony we went to the back room to sign the register accompanied by the witnesses and the photographer. There were cheers and clapping when we left the church and we got covered with confetti. More photos were taken outside and then afterwards we were driven to the pub for our reception.

You could not fault the caterers display and the three-tier cake which was prepared by one of Jill's aunts and stood on a table like an icon.

Let me tell you quickly about her Aunt-Bett. She shared a house with her older sister, Harry's sisters, and they lived in Islington where Jill's family originated from. Her aunt's speciality was cooking, and she used to make the best trifle in the land, also taught Rose. One day Jill and I paid her a visit in Islington and I watched how she was preparing it. With regret, because when she was turning the custard and talking to us at the same time she was smoking and blew the ash from the end of her cigarette which was hanging from her mouth and it fell into the pot; that was the moment I fell out of love with her cooking, especially her trifle.

Going back to our wedding reception and as Jill and I danced she looked up at me with her smiling blue eyes and said.
  "Thank you, my hubby"… "I hope you don't mind me calling you hubby?" … "I've got a lovely present for you and I am dying to give it to you"
  "Thank you, my wife" … "You also don't know how much I am dying to give it to you"
I asked her what it was, she smiled and said.
  "You spoilt it; my surprise was my body is on offer to you"
I replied and said.
  "Sorry can I unwrap it here and now?"
  "I dare you; just remember my dad, brother and uncles are here specially my uncle Billy who is Italian and is married to my mum's sister, do you still want to unwrap me now?"
After looking at them I replied.
  "No, I will give it a rain cheque; I will settle for a kiss right now."

Within two hours the bar ran dry, so Jill's uncles and my friends had a whip round and re-fuelled it.

My mate Micky came over and said.

"I was sweating because I thought you would need me to climb over the wall again."

"No mate" … "It's bloody nice to see you all again" … "By the way do you remember when I told you I am going to marry Jill" … "Remind me, did we ever have that bet?"

"No, we didn't and don't try that on me"

We shook hands and he returned to the others.

After cutting the cake, I said to my mother and Rose.

"Jill wants each of you to take a tier for the Christening and please don't panic there is nothing on the way "YET".

Jill and I went around and thanked everybody, and also, we hoped that they enjoyed our wedding as much as we did. Jill and I decided to leave and went home first to change, then we walked to the underground station with a small case each and got off at Covent Garden station. We carried on walking to the Strand Palace Hotel because it worked out much cheaper on the fare to travel that way.

We arrived and booked in at the reception desk, a porter took our cases and led us to our room. He wished us a happy honeymoon and left. It was one of their first class and the best room on offer. It appeared that one of our guests was a very wealthy foreign business man and a close friend of my father and he upgraded the room without us knowing and told my father that it was our wedding present from him.

Jill said.

"How are we supposed to pay for this?"

"We will scarper in the morning; you run first, and I will follow you"

"Be serious Peter" … "Or shall I call you Coco the clown"

Whilst we were still talking, room service telephoned, I picked it up. They asked me if we liked the room and also, they had a gift for us with the compliments from the management.

I told the girl there has been a mistake and that this was not the room I booked. She replied with a disappointed voice that it was the best they can offer also one of their regular customers who is also a major shareholder has booked it with all expenses paid.

I laughed and said to her.

"Don't tell me his name is Santa."

Within seconds of putting the telephone down there was a knock on the door and a bottle of Champagne in a silver ice bucket was wheeled in and left. I told Jill what was going on after she asked me, and she then said.

"There's someone special up there looking down on us today."

I replied.

"In for a penny in for a pound, when do I get the present you promised me?"

"After I tart myself up for you, and we knock back this bottle of bubbly, because I need gallons of Dutch courage"

I laughed and replied.

"I will order a gallon of Dutch larger for you"

She began to walk away and turned her head round and said.

"Now I am sure I have married a lunatic" … "I only hope you don't get violent."

Jill left the room and after she had a bath came out wearing one of the hotel's white towelling dressing gown with "HER'S" embroidered in gold on it. I was dumb struck when I noticed that she had washed all her make up off and stood in front of me in her natural beauty which was beyond my wildest dreams and she looked like a Madonna.

With a flushed face and an angelic smile, she said.

"Put your eyes back in their socket and stop dribbling, also don't forget your tongue that's hanging out."

We made love for the very first time and it was   pure love without any lust. I apologised for rushing it and she replied that she wasn't ready herself only because she felt scared stiff and didn't know what she was expecting from the experience.

I switched the lights off and tried to sleep. I heard her crying silently and asked her what was wrong.
She replied and said.

"I miss my mum and dad; I am not used to staying away from them that long" ... "I want to go home please, and now"

"Can it wait till the morning, we have return tickets and there are no trains running?"

"I am so sorry just ignore me please, I wish I had your gallon of larger instead of that bloody bubbly"
I gave her a kiss and cuddled her close to my body till the morning.
She woke up first and kissed me then said with a smile.

"Good morning, my very beautiful and not forgetting handsome hubby"
I laughed and replied.

"You can't be my wife because you are more beautiful than her, especially first thing in the morning"

"Shut up; now you are really winding me up."

There was a knock on the door and room service wheeled in a trolley with a full English breakfast.
After we finished, I said to her.

"I hope you can cook as good as this?"
She replied.

"I hope you don't eat as much, because we will go broke within one week."

After we had breakfast, we made love again and it was a great improvement from the previous night; maybe because it was on a full stomach.

We packed our bags and left to reception. The girl asked if everything was alright and to our satisfaction.
Jill replied.

"It was very lovely, and I was satisfied; you should try it one day but not with my husband because he is all mine from now on"

"Thank you; but I am not in your league to have board members of the hotel as my friends"
Jill looked at me and whispered.

"The silly cow obviously doesn't know we're skint."
The doorman came over and took our cases then said.

"Will you please follow me"
I asked him where are we going and he replied that a Rolls Royce is waiting to take us back home.

In our dazed state and as we sat in the back of the car, Jill whispered and said.

"Phew! I thought he was going to nick us because I packed the His and Hers towelling robes in our bags"

"That's very dishonest of you Jill"

"I'm not a thief; after all they did say His and Hers on them"

"You are right" …. "Sorry! I also would never accuse you of being a thief"
I then began to laugh.
She was still not happy with me and said.

"Can anybody else join in with your joke?"

"Yes of course my angel; I also nicked the soap"
We both began to laugh loudly.
Then she said.

"You know hubby I can easily fall in love and get accustomed to this way of life, mind you, with you only that is"

"I promise you that I will make your dreams come true one day"

"Yes, I am sure you will, but I bet there's also a high price to pay if you ever do reach this level."

We arrived home and I went to my pocket to get some change out to tip the driver, but he refused and said that it has already been taken care of. He then wished us a happy life together and was sure that we will do just that, also to wear the gowns often as they will always jog our memories of the one night in the Strand Palace Hotel and drove off laughing.

Rose and Harry welcomed us back and asked how we got on and we told them.

CHAPTER 7

We freshened up and left to see my parents. My mother seemed a little offish, so I asked her what was bothering her.

She said.

"Why have you chosen to live with Jill's parents and not us?"

I replied that her mother still needed help and when she gets stronger, we will temporary move into my old bedroom"

She replied.

"Sorry I'm being selfish; you are right."

Several weeks passed, unfortunately Jill's nan passed away peacefully in her sleep from natural causes at the age of 90.

The night before the funeral Jill and the rest of her family were very upset, also several more relatives stayed the night and shared Jill's bedroom. I decided to stay and sleep on the two-seater settee in the front room and believe it or not I had to share it with nan who was laid in an open coffin in the middle of the room.

I felt very nervous and uncomfortable at first but soon got used to it simply because I never feared nan when she was alive and loved her dearly, so that made it easier.

I managed to eventually go off into a light sleep but was disturbed by noises coming from her coffin. I put the light on and took a closer look. I just couldn't believe my eyes when I saw her smile. Then I automatically smiled back, switched the light off and went into a comfortable deep sleep.

It didn't seem long before Jill knocked on the door and I told her to come in, but she refused because she could not handle the situation. I went to the door and she passed me a cup of coffee through a gap. I told her that I will drink it in the kitchen with her.

When we entered Rose was there preparing breakfast and asked me if I slept well, I told her what happened, then she burst out laughing and said.

"You silly sod that often happens, its wind in the body."

To keep the peace and harmony in the family Jill and I moved in with my parents but unfortunately it didn't work out, so we moved and found in the next road a council house with one bedroom and a small dining room and shared the rest of the facilities with a single middle-aged lady who lived there; cash in hand because she wasn't allowed to sub-let.

The bedroom was truly a BED room because it was so small that the double bed filled up all the space and we had to jump in from the bottom as there was no room on either side.

Jill wasn't happy and kept crying at night. I asked her what was troubling her, and she said nothing because her place was with me and wanted to keep her promise, she made to God on our wedding day.

We were invited to my mother's house for Sunday dinner; Jill left me with my father in the front room and went to see my mother who was in the kitchen preparing the Sunday meal.

On their return they entered the front room and interrupted us. My mother's face was beaming, but Jill's eyes were red, and it seemed as if she was crying.

I asked my mother.

 "Why have you upset Jill again?"

 "Upset? The poor girl is terrified"

I asked Jill what was wrong and if it was me? She replied.

"Sort of you, because you had something to do with it" … "I am still too scared to tell you, your mum will."

With loss of temper, I said.

 "Well come on, one of you spit it out"

My mother replied and said.

 "I won't beat about the bush with you Peter; Jill is pregnant, and you are going to be a dad, also we with Harry and Rose grandparents"

I simply replied.

"What's all the fuss" ... "Is that all?"

Jill's face turned bright red and her angry eyes expressed it all.

When the penny dropped, I shouted out.

 "WHAT!"

I stood up and put my arms around the two of them and began to kiss and cuddle them both and just didn't want to stop or let go.

My father's face beamed with a smile and he stood up and gave Jill a kiss on her forehead.

Jill then said.

 "You don't mind?" ... "I'm so sorry Peter, I've ruined our marriage; where are we going to live now?"

 "It's the best news I have ever heard just let me worry about the rest darling the mother to be to all of our children"

My father went to his writing desk and took out a large brown envelope and then passed it to me.

Jokingly I said.

 "Thanks dad but we can't both move into this envelope it's a little on the small side."

 He was elated and said to me.

 "Open it you clown; you will find Jill's answer in it"

It was a certificate for an endowment policy which he took out when I was born, and it was worth £2,000.

He then carried on saying.

 "Your brother also has one." ... "What I would like to suggest to you is buy a good second-hand cheap car and then with the balance use it to get a mortgage; it will be a good start in your young lives; also buy sooner rather than later because the housing market is going to shoot up sky high, and beyond expectation."

With joy I kissed him; he was not used to receiving affection because he was still a Victorian in his ways and pulled a face of disgust, but still thanked me.

The next day which was a Monday, Jill and I walked to the station and travelled to our work on the same train as per usual. When we reached the third station Jill asked if we could get off because she felt sick and was. We then caught the next train and history repeated itself as she asked again, and we got off and caught the next. I decided that under no circumstances will I allow her to carry on travelling on her own, so I stayed with her till she arrived to her place of work and agreed to wait outside when she finished in the evening and then we will travel back home together because hubby wants to look after baby and mother. She was okay on our return journey home.

When we got there and on our way home, I suggested that we will go and visit her parents because they also have the right to know about the baby.

She said that her dad will kill her.

I laughed and replied that she was a married woman and also not to be a drama queen.

We had a quick bite and left to her parent's house.

As soon as we entered Rose kept staring at Jill; call it motherly instinct.

She then said to her.

"Have you got anything to tell me?"

With slight anger Jill replied.

"Has Peter's mum been round and opened her big gob again?"

"No, she hasn't; you've jumped the gun again. How long have you known?"

"Only yesterday mum" … "Besides we are here to tell you" Rose with tears of joy went over to her and they both began to sob then hugged and kissed each other. Harry was standing nearby, and looked extremely confused, and then asked.

"I know I'm a bit thick, but have I missed out on anything?"

We all looked at him and burst out laughing.

Jill went over and hugged, then kissed him and placed his hand on her stomach and said.

"Say hello to your grandchild"

Harry looked at Peter and said.

"Cor blimey! I never knew you had it in ya"

I smiled and thought.

"Correction Harry, more in Jill"

Jill told her mother about the morning sickness and she advised her not to take any pills to prevent it as it may harm the baby and the problem of being sick will soon solve itself.

Jill and I carried on life as normal and we rekindled our friendship with Allan who married Linda. I went with Allan and traded my old car in to an updated brown Morris Minor as my father suggested. Also, with help from my friend, I managed to pass my driving test the first time because he knew the examiner well and owed him a favour.

In the meantime, Jill and I went house hunting and found a small two bedroomed with a bathroom front room and sitting room come kitchen; by the way the kitchen was a Butler Sink in the recess to the right as you enter the room.

The owner was a single young man in his thirties and told us that he inherited it from his aunt but was living with a male partner who disliked the property. Also, he himself wasn't happy living there because it brought back memories of his aunt which he loved dearly and needed a quick sale as he and his partner were moving out of the area and up market.

He was asking £1,990 and told us that he will not take one penny less for it.

Jill fell madly in love with the property although it was small like a dolls house.

I told her that we could not go to his asking price because it needed a lot of work, so we decided to leave to look at the next property on our list.

As I opened the front door, he called us back and said.

"Do you really like the property Jill?"

She answered.

"Like it! I just love it! But we can't go to your asking price because I am expecting our first baby and we need extra money for it."

"You know my aunt would have loved to hear you say that because she also loved this house; how much can you afford and please don't come up with a silly offer?"

I interrupted and said.

"£1700."

"It's all yours for the asking, on one condition you will have to clear my auntie's furniture"

"It's a deal"

I replied and we shook hands on it.

Jill went over and gave him a kiss and a hug.

He blushed and responded with laughter then said to her.

"Thank God my Roger isn't here to witness you do that to me, he would scratch your eyes out sweet darling Jill."

Jill and I left, and we felt elated and sat in our car to recover from the ordeal; she leaned over and gave me a kiss.

I asked her what was that for?

She said.

"The hug and kiss which I gave him was only to make sure he didn't change his mind about the deal"

"I am so sorry to disappoint you sweet darling Jill, and can assure you that he dealt after he touched my flesh when we shook hands"

She in short, replied.

"Big Head" … "I hope you're not serious?"

That purchase was our first step up the ladder.

We returned home and went to my parent's first. Jill cuddled and kissed my parents and then thanked them. We then left to tell her parents the good news which was received with mixed feelings by them. One was that we have our own home which made them feel very happy but the other, disappointed because we are going to move further away from them.

Rose looked at me and said.

"Listen very carefully to me Peter and always remember that going up the ladder in life is hard, but what is harder is to stay up there especially when you reached the top; God forbid if you have to come down again, they will be waiting for you; so, try to stay clean whilst climbing and may be one or two so called friends if ever you come down will sympathise with you and that's all you will get from them"

"Thank you Rose, that's what I call good advice."

We managed to finalise the purchase and one of my father's close friends who was a solicitor did the deal free of charge and said it was his belated wedding present to us. We didn't need a removable lorry because all our possessions were transported in her father's and our car.

Our marriage was taking a new chapter for the better as per our vows. I told Jill to take the day off work because I noticed that she was so excited about her new home and wanted to give it a spring clean. I reminded her that she was pregnant before I left and told her not to overdo it, then left to work on my own.

Amazing as it may sound it was my very first day I travelled alone and without her, I felt lost and lonely as if my right arm had dropped off.
I hurried home that evening and was greeted at the door by my beautiful, pregnant and domesticated wife who was wearing a blue scarf on her head and short of a cigarette hanging from her mouth, mind you luckily, she didn't smoke.

We cuddled and kissed at the door, she then said
  "I missed you madly today, but you are just about to witness what a perfect wife you have married."
She turned around smiled and pointed behind her, then with a loud voice said.
  "TRALAAA!"
I was very impressed because not only the house was tidy it also smelled fresh, clean and homely and said to her.
  "Well done darling" … "Did you do all this hard work by yourself?"
  "No, silly, as if I would, my mum and dad gave me a hand."
  "OH! Good. Tell me, what did you do with all the antique furniture the aunt left behind?"
She began to laugh then blew warm breath on her finger nails, rubbed them against her body and proudly replied.

"I did a deal with the rag and bone man and gave him only 2 quid which my dad loaned me to take all that old junk away, by the way the council wanted a fiver."

I slapped my forehead with the palm of hand and with loss of temper replied.

"WHAT! I just don't believe I heard that, please darling say that you are just winding me up"

She burst out crying and shouted back at me.

"You are one spoiled and ungrateful sod, I suppose you could've done better and only gave him one quid"

I didn't like to see her upset and said.

"Don't cry darling you didn't know; besides it was my fault for not telling you." … "Just for the record did you know what you gave away was worth more than the house is: I was going to get one of my old mate's father to auction them for us in his next sale" … "Oh, well, never mind there's still one consolation, I left old original Victorian oil paintings under the stairs and they are still worth a lot money"

She burst out crying again and said.

"That's it, I am going to pack my bag and go back home to my mum, you see I found them and also gave them to him"

I sat at the bottom of the stairs and burst out laughing instead of sobbing my heart out, only after seeing the funny side of the situation and she quickly joined me with broken sobs.

We decided to forget the error and then kissed and made up (best part by the way and that was worth the loss).

CHAPTER 8

Jill and I got on well together in our marriage, we were very happy and contented; our main goal then was to see our firstborn baby. The reason behind our successful marriage was we loved and cared for one another and never got bored in each other's company because we just could not get enough of it. Mind you we also did have the occasional disagreement only because we were complete opposites and that also seemed to have worked out well for us.

We didn't have much spare cash for luxuries, in a matter of fact very little and managed on one wage because the journey was getting very tiring for Jill so we decided that she should give it up. I was still working in the City for the tea company and soon moved up and became third in line for manager with an increased wage to £15 a week. Although we had a car, we walked everywhere to economise.

To make ends meet, Rose and Harry kept treating us to the occasional tinned food and gave us their old television because they bought a new one and also my mother and father gave us a deposit for a Cyril Lord carpet for our bedroom. I was extremely grateful to them but wasn't very happy, because I wanted to give my wife and future child a more luxurious life with my efforts and burning ambition.

I decided to work in the evening in a football pool's company which was a walking distance from our house and Jill with help from a family friend got her homework making Masonic aprons. With our extra income we paid for a hallway and stairs carpet on HP and within six months we managed to clear our debts.

By then Jill was getting very large and nearer to her time. My mother invited us down for a meal, it was a pleasant Summer evening and after dinner Jill and I decided to take their dog Prince out for a walk. As we reached the exact spot where Jill and I first met another dog passed and Prince took a dislike to him and pulled Jill over. She was shocked and shaken also worried about the baby. We returned to my mother's and left in our car to go home.

On our way back Jill said that she had cramping pains in her stomach, so I stopped at our GP and he suggested that I took her to the nearest hospital which was in Hanley Road, Finsbury Park, although there was another only a five minutes' walk away from us, but it didn't have the facilities to examine Jill and the baby. She was rushed into the delivery room on our arrival although she still had three weeks to go. There were complications with the after-birth but they managed to get the situation under control and our first also very beautiful baby girl was born. I managed to get the news to the rest of the family and there was almost a stampede of visitors to the hospital.

The baby got spoilt silly by our friends and family also not forgetting Jill and I. You know never move near a pub because you will always be visiting it regularly and the ruling in my opinion also applies to a hospital and we had one a walking distance from our house.

Number two arrived and she was born a year after and then the following year the third, another beautiful girl was born. This one was different she had blue eyes and blonde hair and looked almost a replica of Jill.

Nothing good comes easy and cheap in life and we nearly had a high price to pay for that baby; during her delivery Jill's blood pressure climbed to hypertension stage 2 and began to clot. Miraculously they managed to bring it down. After her discharge Jill and I decided to walk back home as it was near, and I carried the baby. On our way I was joking after noticing that the baby was different from the other two and said to Jill.
  "I hope we've come away with the right baby"
She laughed and replied.

"You are becoming one greedy sod; am I not entitled to at least have one of my babies looking like me?"

"Just this one, the next will have to be a handsome good-looking boy, and I don't have to emphasize further like who."

You have all guessed right, just under a year and half number four arrived. Another addition to the family and another beautiful; guess what? I will put you out of your misery; a girl.

Life with four lovely girls was priceless and they were growing up fast. Winter arrived and it was a very severe one. It was named Siberian weather because it was a very bitter and cold period. We were struggling with our bills at the time and one night we decided to bring down to the front room our mattress and the six of us huddled together on the floor to keep warm. It was very cosy and warm until I woke up in the middle of the night and felt cold water dripping down on my face from the ceiling light. A pipe had burst and flooded the room. In the morning and by sheer luck we had a young builder living next door, he came in and fixed the pipe and then told us to claim off the house insurance for the carpets.

One Saturday Jill was really down in the dumps, so to cheer her up I decided to surprise her and the children. I told her that I won't be long just going to Wood Green. She told me to drive carefully because the roads were icy, and we didn't need any more problems right now.
I went to a pet shop and bought her favourite dog, a spotted Dalmatian and picked it up at a very cheap price, also the shop keeper assured me that it was a thoroughbred.

I returned home and felt over the moon because I was just about to please and cheer my wife and children up. I knocked on the door, Jill opened it, and her eyes nearly popped out of their sockets.

She spoke with a raised and angry voice...very angry voice and said.

"What the bloody hell have you got there?"

I replied with a big smile on my face and said.

"It's your favourite dog darling, a Dalmatian; do you like it?"

"She slammed the door in my face, even the dog stopped wagging his tail and looked up at me with a surprised look on his face.

With a begging voice I said.

"Please Jill let us in, it's bloody cold out here"

I could hear the girls saying to her.

"Oh, please mum, we love him let the dog in and leave daddy out he is naughty"

Jill was adamant and gave me no other alternative then she shouted back.

"Get rid of that bloody dog, and don't bother to come back until you do"

I replied "It's a thoroughbred Jill"

"Cor blimey, I thought you had brains Peter; the bloke in the shop saw you coming, that's a bloody mongrel and I bet the spots have been painted on it"

I returned to the pet shop and confronted the man and told him that my wife said it's a mongrel and not a thoroughbred Dalmatian.

He replied.

"I never said it's a thoroughbred and if you listened carefully, I said it's thoroughly bred; besides once an animal leaves these premises, we can't take them back" ... "Look at the sign up there its clear enough"

A young boy about 11 years old tugged at my arm and said.

"He sold me this budgie as well mister and my mum told me to take it back and get my birthday money which he nicked of me, so that she can put more towards it for a dog, but he won't"

I forgot about my own problem and felt sorry for the boy, so as we were both in the same boat, I suggested to him.

"I will do a deal with you; lets swap"

Without any hesitation the boy said.

"Yeah, it's a deal mister"

I returned home and knocked on door.

Jill peaked through a gap with her foot on the other side to prevent me from opening it further and asked.

"Did you get rid of that dog?"

"Yes"

She opened the door and burst out laughing at the sight of the bird in its cage and said.

"You are a sight for sore eyes, I thought you would never come back" … "Come on in with your new friend."

I replied.

"Thank you darling, I promise to take it out for a walk every day"

Jill said sarcastically.

"I will also promise you that I will let it out without a lead if it gets hard work when you are not here."

The girls went berserk with excitement when they saw the bird. Unfortunately, the budgie passed away three weeks after because it went past its sell by date.

Allan and Linda came around one night with a couple of beers and a small bottle of gin with a can of orange juice to celebrate their wedding anniversary with us. By the way that's how many drank gin in those days. I was in conversation with Allan and he asked me.

"How much do you recon your house is worth now?"

I replied.

"About 4 grand why are you asking?"

"No way mate"

I betted him that I may even get more for it.

Jill interrupted us and said.

"Why don't you put your money where your mouth is and prove it to your mate, besides this place is getting too small for us"

"Right you two, it goes on the market on Monday."

I found a local estate agent on the Monday and after a valuation of £4,500, Jill and I agreed that we should go for it and buy a larger house, but it will still have to be within reach of our parents.

Within one week the very first buyers who viewed it agreed to pay the asking price after we turned down their offer. It left us dizzy because we had to move fast to find property to comply and complete and also move out within five weeks.

My eldest sister who lived in Edmonton got in touch with us and said that one of her neighbours was selling their modern three-bedroom semi-detached house and we could do a deal directly with them and save Agents fees.

We went to view it; one always knows if the home they are buying is the right one because you get an unmistakable feeling of love, warmth and comfort as soon as you enter it. We made the deal and bought the house for £4,850 and borrowed extra on our mortgage to have it carpeted and decorated also splashed out and bought new clothes for us and the children and treated our parents to a small present each.

That was a further step up the ladder for us.

CHAPTER 9

New house new baby; yes, Jill was really having a swelling time (excuse the pun) and became pregnant again.

The baby was a run of our mill with her beautiful looks and had blonde hair with blue eyes; in case you have lost count, she was number 5.

Jill's parents moved out of Wood Green to Enfield which was about three miles away from our new home.

In the mean time I was doing very well in City and my income increased because I was promoted to assistant export manager after the retirement of the present one and bought a second-hand five-seater car.

We became one big happy and loving inseparable family and we spent a lot of time together whenever we could and often visited zoos, funfairs, the seaside and even spent a week in a Holiday Camp and took a boat out on the Norfolk Broads. They were truly happy and trouble-free days.

Everybody gets a setback in their lives and ours was when I was called into my manager's office and he told me to go immediately to my mother's house because my father suffered a heart attack. He recovered but could not return to his shipping business on his doctor's orders.
My older brother by then was demobbed from the Air Force and he and his wife took over my father's business and made a mess of it because he was a qualified air mechanic and neither of them had a clue about export and shipping or running a business.

My mother begged me to leave the City because my father's health had a setback due to the problems which were beginning to mount up in his troubled business. I discussed the matter with Jill and told her that its going to be a great risk to take; she simply said family come first and if it wasn't for your father where would we be today. I told her that I would agree, but we have five growing up children and I need my work to pay our own bills also my manager said that he is soon retiring, and the opportunity is vast for me, also reminded me that the company is one of the strongest in the country.

Jill replied.

"I am sorry Peter I can't give you my opinion simply because I just don't know what the risk is, but always remember through thick or thin I will always love you and stand by you, for richer or for poorer because you are my hero now and always will be until my dying day."

She stopped and laughed then carried on saying.

"Mind you the last bit I just said is if I die before you that is."

I took the biggest gamble in my life and left the City and the friends I made there, then took over my father's ailing business.

After studying the figures with his accountant, we found out that he was in debt and owed the bank over £4,000 and the most sensible action to take was to liquidate the business otherwise my parents would lose their house.

I discussed it with my father, he agreed that the risk I am taking will be very high. I was torn and could not make up my mind which way to turn.

When I went home that evening Jill came into the room wearing the HERS towelling robe, I began to laugh because I knew she was trying to cheer me up.

She looked stunning and irresistible.

My laughter turned to a smile and I said.

"Just stay away from me please, we can't afford number 6 yet"

She replied.

"Trying is just as good you know."

"You have just given me an idea which will save us all from making any mistakes"

She began to laugh and replied.

"Forget it, I am a good girl and my dad just wouldn't agree to see or allow me to go on the game."
She was right it was a wonderful night.

I left the next morning to my father's office and his secretary told me that Mr Sami telephoned to find out how your father was, and he also would like to meet up with you and your lovely wife Jill at the Strand Palace hotel for dinner and to meet his wife who will also be there as well.
I telephoned home and told Jill about the invitation, but she declined it because she said that she didn't have anything decent to wear.
I told her to wear the towelling robe she nicked from his hotel.
She simply replied.
  "You are sick hubby"
When I got home, Rose opened the door; I gave her a kiss on the cheek and asked her where Jill was, and she told me that she was upstairs getting ready to impress and kill without taking any prisoner, also she is going to make sure that the foreign business client doesn't get fresh with her, so she has decided to take the five children with her.

I poured myself out a whisky and took a glass in for Harry who was watching the television in the sitting room with the girls. You know our girls absolutely adored and loved him and so did he them.

The room brightened up when my dancing queen entered. She was stunning and stood in front of me, like a goddess, and more beautiful than an English rosebud just about to blossom. She then placed one hand on her hip and posed like a catwalk model and with a sexy voice said.
  "How do I look boys?"
Jokingly I replied.
  "Just like a run of the mill tart"
Harry interrupted us and said to me.
  "It's a bloody wonder she keeps losing it with ya"… "Now tell her she looks stunning"

I said to Jill.
 "Your dad just said that you look stunning"
She laughed and replied.
 "Thanks dad at least you still got a good taste."

I asked Jill if I should drive and she told me that Mr Sami telephoned and told her that he is sending his Roller to pick us up. She went on and said
 "Hey! Just listen to this Peter, he also said that he is looking forward to seeing me!"
We were picked up and as the car stopped outside our house our neighbours came out to be nosey and when they saw the uniformed chauffer open the door for us, they were left extremely impressed.

On the way the driver looked into his driving mirror and said.
 "May I take the liberty and say how beautiful you look Jill; by the way do you still wear the HERS towelling robe?"
 "Thank you and yes, with some regret now and wish I burnt it a long time ago."

We arrived and entered the hotel and were met by Mr Sami who greeted us both with hugs and kisses and led us to a private room where he introduced us to his wife who was dressed in an elegant long black silk dress. She was stunning and friendly but still not a touch on my Jill.

I kept looking at my wife, I was still madly in love with her and felt so proud, especially by the way she handled herself in an environment which was new to her.
Whilst the girls chatted to each other Mr Sami and I discussed business. It seemed that my father and he had already spoken to each other regarding the discussion were having. He told me that he is willing to take me under his wings because he needed a reliable and honest man to look after his shipments and purchases from the UK.
I told him I feel very honoured by his offer but unfortunately the business is in a mess and I need to clean it up first, then

I wouldn't hesitate but to accept his precious offer if ever he asked me the second time.

He smiled and replied.

"That is a very good example of honesty but let me advise you; sometimes in the real   business world you have to bluff. Your Golden Gates have just opened so don't close them because unless you are extremely lucky, they may not open a second time for you"

He then took out a cheque already made out in my name for the sum of £10,000 and said.

"This is equal to one spin on a roulette table for me, please don't be offended by it; it will help you and your father out. I am off to the Middle East tomorrow; nice to have you on board Peter"

"Thank you is not enough Mr Sami; you will not regret your decision"

"I have very few regrets in my life; I have a good wife like you have Jill and also blessed with healthy children; that's why I am where I am today."

We returned home again in his Rolls Royce, but I never told Jill what happened.

I told Harry and Rose to stop over as it was too late for them to drive back home, also Harry was six sheets in the wind.

I was so excited that night and could not sleep.

Jill noticed and asked me.

"What's up Peter, I hope I didn't let you down tonight?"

"Let me down; you must be joking you were bloody marvellous throughout" … "You know Jill, life with you and my children is a fairy tale my love. I know you will never ever let me down even if you tried; mind you it would be hell and I would be lost if you ever stopped loving me."

CHAPTER 10

The next morning, I left to work whilst Jill was still in conversation with her parents; she just couldn't get her sentences out quick enough as she was telling them about the meeting and dinner.

I had a very important call to make first on my way and popped in on my parents. My father although didn't look very well, he seemed excited and was expecting me.

I asked him should I take Mr Sami's offer?

He replied.

"You are a good man Peter and deserve the best because your heart is in the right place and with Jill behind you, nothing is going to stop you; you're still young and ambitious and will take risks; what you have on offer is an opportunity of a life time, take it and now. I would ask for only one favour in return, please look after your mother after I have gone"

"Thank you, father, but you're not going anywhere except where I am going to send you." … "Amazing as it may sound to you, I really think you are a wise old man with the wisdom of King Solomon. I don't want you to take an offence by what I am just about to say to you; I would like you and mother to go on a cruise all expenses will be paid by me with Jill's blessings"

After arguing it out I won the battle and they both agreed to go.

I left my parent's home and returned to work.

I took a few minutes off and walked to the post office and opened a National Savings account in Jill's name and deposited a £500 cheque in it. Afterwards, I went to my bank which was a short distance away and special cleared the £10,000 cheque which Mr Sami gave me.

Yes, truly Jill and I were on our way up that beautiful ladder of success.

By then our five girls were growing up and the eldest was 9 years old. The business began to flourish, and my account was getting bigger which made a change to Jill's tummy.

We had a heart-breaking set back because Rose went down with the dreaded cancer again. She and Harry moved in with us so that Jill could take care of her. It was a hopeless situation as she became weaker.

I decided to spoil her big time. Every time she fancied anything, I got it for her.

She used to crave for jellied eels and also pie and mash with liquor; by the way that was not alcohol it was a green pea sauce and she insisted only from Tubby Isaac's in the East End. I would go there on my way home and buy it for her.

She would only take one bite and leave the rest.

She lost a lot of weight and was in continuous pain.

She used to beg Jill and I to let her go into a care home because our house was too small, also she felt it was unfair on the children to witness the unpleasant things in life, but we both refused her request.

Jill and I were shopping with the children one day and we decided to treat them. After taking them to the cinema we went on to an ice-cream bar and spoiled them silly.

It was the best time we both could ever remember because it was also the first time we spent together alone as a family for a very long time.

The girls were laughing and singing in the car on our way back and I decided to join them, but Jill soon stepped in and asked me if I could whistle instead.

When we arrived home, we noticed Harry was in the sitting room crying and wiping his eyes on his handkerchief.

Jill asked him what was wrong, and he told her that some family members arranged to take Rose to a home in Hampstead.

Jill and I blew our tops and I said.

"Right Jill, you and I will immediately go and bring her back"

But Harry insisted that it was the best place for her to be and she will get the best treatment possible.

Although business wise everything was going well, we became sad and extremely unhappy as a family.

Jill and her sister were by their mother's bed side every day and we almost became strangers.

Harry looked after the children during the day when I was working and then I took over in the evening to give him a break so that he could visit Rose.

I dosed off in front of the television one Friday night and was disturbed by one of the girls who passed me the telephone.

It was my mother on the line in a frantic state.

I asked her what was wrong, and she said quick your father is not feeling very well and is insisting on seeing you.

I sent one of the girls round to my sister who lived in the same road to fetch her so that she could look after the children.

I left and drove to my parents' home, but I was too late; my father had already passed away with a massive heart attack with the white Persian cat which I bought him for his birthday by his side on the bed.

I felt devasted and left with tears in my eyes after two of my sisters and brother turned up and returned home.

On my arrival my sister asked me how he was, and I told her.

She began to cry and scream in front of the children and left them terrified.

The next day after work I went to pick Jill up from the care home and saw Rose.

I gave her a kiss and she told me not to rush away because she missed our chats.

The first thing she asked.

  "How is your father?"

I lied, held back my tears and replied

  "He's fine Rose and sends you his regards with mother"

She nodded her head and said.

"You're not a good liar" ... "I must tell you what happened today" ... "I went out in the hallway as you come in and to my right, I noticed these stairs; so being nosey I went up them, it was an effort Peter, but I took my time and managed to get to the top. I then opened the door and a blinding warm and comforting light shone in my face. It was so lovely, and all my pain seemed to have disappeared; you know Peter I felt as if I was a teenager again."

I stopped her and went to have a look for myself but to the right was nothing but a grey wall and returned but did not pursue the conversation.

That night about midnight Harry telephoned and told us that Rose had passed.

What a disastrous period in our lives because we had two funerals on our hands in one week.

To add to our misery Jill told me that she missed her periods for two months and just couldn't handle another pregnancy, so we went to the Elizabeth Garrett, now UCL Hospital in Euston Road for a termination.

With Rose gone Jill and I decided that Harry can stay with us as long as he wished.

The three bedroomed house was getting too small, so Jill and I decided to buy a bigger house and we put a deposit on a plot for a townhouse in Wellington Road, Enfield and in the meantime, we moved in with Harry until it was completed.

CHAPTER 11

Our new home was finally built, and the purchase completed, and we moved in. Although we were pleased, at the same we were deprived of the happiness it deserved because the pain and loss in the family was still alive.

You know people say time is a healer, that is not true; time only camouflages, but the pain which is imbedded in your brain and heart unfortunately will never go away and it will leave you scarred for life.

The business was growing faster than what I could cope with and I was forced to employ extra staff. The bigger it grew the less I saw of my wife and children.

One day I had lunch with Mr Sami and during our conversation he told me that I looked tired and added that this was the price one pays for success, because you have to marry your business to stay at the top.

Being left alone with the girls and her father, Jill was finding it difficult to cope with the loss of her mother and the termination. She began to drink heavily and often turned on me for the least thing, also short of holding me responsible for her problems.
I couldn't blame her because I was selfish and also still hungry for more success, it was like injecting adrenalin in my veins.

I began to go out "pubbing it" with the boys on Friday nights.
It started that I used to return home around 9 or 10 o'clock and then I began to turn up in the early hours of the morning and she often used to lock me out and I had to sleep in my car.

I was sitting with my friends in the pub one night and all of a sudden reality hit me.

I looked around me and saw nothing but down and outs, layabouts and drunks.

They were empty and also lost souls going nowhere.

I stood up and drove home.

The journey seemed ever ending because all I wanted was the love of my life Jill and the girls.

I got home and the front door was locked with all the lights out.

I took it out on the door and kept banging it, the whole neighbourhood heard me and shouted out of their windows to stop the noise, except Jill, or did she not hear me?

So, I decided to sleep in the car, but not for long because she came out, tapped on the glass and let me in.

I apologised profusely to her and promised to change my way. Also, from that moment on where ever she went, I would go too.

She kissed me and said.

"Welcome back home my hubby, I missed you and nearly lost you."

The marriage was on the mend and life began to be so amazingly pleasant and full of love again.

I came home after work early on a Friday because I promised to take Jill out to a local Jazz club with Allan and is wife Linda. Jill loved dancing and boy did she move on that floor especially when she mastered the traditional jive, she deliberately wobbled her sexy bum to tease me.

I noticed a glitter in her eyes that night and told her how lovely she looked also, I had missed that smile on her face, actually I missed all smiles when I was out boozing with the boys.

She replied.

"I went out with my friend and bought you your Christmas present"

I was surprise and replied.

"It's only April Jill, what's the hurry"

"Tut.Tut.Tut. It takes 9 months altogether to get it ready, or have you forgotten?"

It didn't take me long to get her message.

We kissed and cuddled on the dance floor, and it felt just like old times.

I asked her.

"I've lost count how many does that make it now?"

"Let me think"… "Oh, yes half a dozen, and that's your lot mate"

"I am going out with your dad tomorrow to buy a minibus"

Then I said can we keep this a secret from Allan and Linda because it will spoil his night when she starts demanding his body.

The next morning Harry and I went car hunting and I decided to buy the latest Ford Zephyr a huge saloon with bench seats in the front and back and it could easily seat 6 to 7 passengers.

I noticed that Harry was interested in a Ford Escort and bought it for him, that made his day and he said with a saddened face.

"I wish Rose was still here to see this; TA, very much son"… "I honestly just don't know what to say?"… "You know I feel as if Christmas is already here"

"Thank you, Harry, amazing as it may sound to you, but I also feel exactly the same and my main present is coming on the actual day later on in the year"

I settled the purchases with the car salesman and we both drove home.

I was driving in front of Harry and could see him in the mirror. His face was beaming with a smile and he looked as happy as a sandboy.

When we arrived back, Jill and the girls came out and jumped in the car and then insisted that I took them round the block.

Jill sat closer to me on the bench seat and said.

"I have never seen my dad look so happy; thank you for that."

When we got back home, we heard a knock on our front door's letter box.

I opened it but could not see anybody there until I felt a tug on my trousers.

It was a little blonde boy dressed in his grey school uniform; one of our neighbour's son.

I crouched down to his level and asked him.

"What can I do for you young man?"

He wiped his running nose on his shirt sleeve and said.

"Can the girls come out to play?"

I began to laugh and replied that they were doing their homework, but I will pass his message on.

He began to walk away with a disappointed look on his face and then turned around, smiled and said.

"Do you want to come out instead?"

"Another time"… "What's your name by the way?"

"It's Kevin"… "And what's your?"

"Peter."

I went and told Jill about him and she said that he often knocked on the door, also all the girls loved him.

Being pregnant again Jill decided to cut out on her G & T's and that made a lot of difference to her behaviour, she began to drink only white wine in moderation.

Christmas arrived but my present didn't. Jill went in the local private hospital and on the 27th of December baby six arrived unwrapped.

I rushed with the five girls to her bedside, and on the way to the ward we passed her doctor.

He acknowledged us and then began to laugh loudly and said.

"Don't bother to ask Peter, but does Baby Emma give you a clue?"

Jill and the baby had a check-up and were discharged early. We celebrated with continuous visitors till New Year's Eve and it was tiring but fun.

Jill and I were one evening upstairs in the sitting room when the dust had settled after the birth of number six and listening to music, she asked me if the business was still doing well and I told her that it couldn't get any better, also why was she asking.

"When I went for a check-up with my dad today, we went past this fantastic detached house; you would just love it Peter"

"Why don't you like this one anymore?"

"I love it but being a townhouse, I am finding it hard work to keep going up and down those stairs."

Jill got her way as per usual and after giving me extra affection, we bought the house which was upmarket and just off the Ridgeway.

By then the sixth baby who was also another beautiful girl was two years old. We didn't see much of the five eldest ones because they spend a lot of time sleeping over and playing with their friends. They were happy and that was the most important thing.

CHAPTER 12

Jill struck a friendship with a woman her own age whom she met when shopping at Harrods in the West End. She lived about three miles away from us in Hadley Wood, a stock brokers belt area.

After visiting her one-day Jill returned home looking very excited. I was beginning to dread that unmistakable approach because it meant one of two things; she was pregnant, or we are on the move again. The latter was my preferential and I waited for the bomb shell to be dropped and it wasn't long before it did when she began to speak and said.

"Do you still remember my friend Joan who lives in Hadley Wood, well...."
I stopped her and with a sign of relief on my face laughed and said.

"She's pregnant?"
She replied.

"No, Mr Clever-boots" ... "See you don't know everything"
"Come on Jill, the suspense is killing me, please spit it out"
"Two doors up to where she lives there are a very rich old couple, and they are moving to their house by the sea in Frinton" ... "It needs an extension and has nearly one acre of land overlooking farm land and backing on to the golf course; I will let you play golf if we move there"
This by the way is why Jill had 6 children, because I just couldn't refuse her anything.

We sold and this was a very nervous move for me because we were now reaching the top of our ladder and I remembered what Rose told me, that it would be much harder to stay there.

When we moved in, we had to spend a small fortune on the property to get it to Jill's standard and taste which by now was getting expensive and up-market. Also, it was her department and she knew exactly what she was doing.

We ended up with a little mansion of 8 bedrooms, three bathrooms, two reception rooms and a very large kitchen with a dining area to seat 16 people.

In addition to the blue stag drop head car which I bought her for her birthday I took her and bought her another car and this time it was a Porsche.

Life was wonderful at the top, but extremely hectic and exhausting. We had regular parties, visiting casinos with clients until the earlier hours and going abroad regularly. I kept my promise to Jill though that where ever she went, I went too, within reason by the way.

Her cousin from Wood Green had moved to Bedford. Her husband was a window cleaner by trade; however, he had become involved in buying and selling silver and his luck had changed. They came to visit us one day and fell in love with the area and decided to move near us.

Five of the girls got married and we gave them each the best which money could buy, together with a deposit for a house and a car.
Baby Emma was still living at home, when she was in that is because she spent most of her time out with her friends from the convent school which she attended. The nuns spent a lot of their spare time drinking my sherry when visiting us at home and that was often and enjoyable.

I came home one evening feeling extremely tired, Jill opened the door.
She was intoxicated and very angry and shouted.
"And who is the red-headed tart you've been with?"
I was shocked and shouted back.
  "For God's sake Jill have you gone mad or been on something stronger than Gin?"
  "I had a telephone call from a girl who said that you are carrying on and she saw you"

"The only redhead I know and dine with midday is my secretary and you know that, also our relationship is strictly business."

She grabbed hold of her mother's Waterford fruit bowl which was nearby on a table and threw it at me; I ducked, and it missed me by inches, and then it hit the wall and shattered.

I made one very big mistake and laughed.

She was still fuming in temper and said.

"So, you think that was funny" ... "See if this will also make you laugh."

She began to sob her heart out and carried on saying.

"You bastard; you made me break my mums favourite bowl"

She left the house and went to the front drive, got into her Triumph Stag sports car and reversed it to the top, then put her foot down and rammed the second love in my life which was my Panther Lima sports car, a replica of a vintage Morgan; by the way Jill was my first and only true love besides my girls.

She reversed to repeat her vicious attack on my car, so to stop her I stood in front of her car and told her to carry on, also I wasn't going to move out of the way.

Harry came to my rescue and pulled her out of the car, that gave me time to open the bonnet on the Stag and remove the distributor head.

Harry asked me what the hell is going on and why was she in that state.

I told him about the telephone call she got.

He didn't seem very surprised and said that he also picked up the phone several times before and the same girl told him about me and the redhead.

We went in and I poured out two whiskies and also a Gin and T for Jill.

We sat down calmly to discuss the matter further.

Miracles do happen, the phone rang, and Jill picked it up.

It was the same girl again and told Jill.

"If you come right now to the Finsbury Park Hotel you will see your hubby with the redhead whom I've been trying to warn you about"

"Thank you; whilst you are about it could you also do me one very big favour darling and tell her to keep him" … "By the way without seeing you I bet you've got cheap dyed red hair. Now just do yourself a favour and piss off you mad cow because my husband happens to be here and sitting right in front of me"

Jill then slammed the phone down.

She then looked at her glass of Gin and T and put it down on the table without sipping it and began to cry and apologise to me.

I stopped her and said.

"There are many jealous and poisonous hissing snakes out there Jill, always think first, analyse the situation before taking any action"

She replied by saying.

"I am so sorry; I love you very much and get very jealous, and also I don't want to lose you unless you tell me that you want to walk out on me"… "I promise that I will make it up to you somehow"

Harry took a long sip from his glass and said.

"Do you two mind if I stay here right now because I am not prepared to go anywhere just in case you two start on number 7"

His statement soon changed the atmosphere in the room from doom and gloom, to joy and happiness because he was serious and made us burst out with laughter.

CHAPTER 13

My mother passed away and that was another sad and dark day in our lives. I arranged for her funeral and she was laid in the same grave as my father's.
She got a good farewell; I stood the expenses and told Jill to make sure that nothing but the best for her.

I didn't go to her funeral because I was getting tired of losing loved ones and decided to stay at home and grieve on my own. Also, I didn't want my girls to witness me in a weak state because they always looked on at me as their pillar of strength in their lives.

Harry went with Jill and the girls and their husbands. He was extremely upset because they got on well together over the years. He and Rose with my father and mother often spent happy holidays abroad together.

The passing away of my mother was natural which all families have to face up to one day and must try to accept it; I also know it is a time when one generation takes over from the other, mind you it's easier to say that than to accept.

There was a rift in my family afterwards because I had stayed away from my mother's funeral. The true feelings of how my sisters and brother felt about me surfaced as they used my absence from the funeral as a snub to them and an insult to my mother.

I personally think they took this opportunity to punish me for my success in the business which they thought was the same business my father had handed to me. However, it wasn't, and they conveniently forgot how I had kept them all when he was alive and had carried on looking after my mother, as I had promised my father, since he had passed away. I had paid my mother's bills and gave her a weekly income, also saved her house which at that time they stood to inherit.

CHAPTER 14

Life went back to normality; my wife and I fell deeper in love as every day passed. She and I spent a lot of time travelling abroad for our holidays and often took some of the girls with us.

It was just another lovely and warm summer's evening and after work Jill and I, with Harry, sat in the back garden and had a Turkish take-away, it was a change from Indian and Chinese.

The telephone rang and I answered it.
It was Mr Sami on the other end and sounded extremely disturbed.
I asked him what was wrong.
He replied.
  "Bad news Peter, we are BROKE my dear friend"
I shouted back.
  "What?"
He told me that the last big deal we did with Africa went horribly wrong and we will not get paid because the government has gone broke and all banks have been closed.
I returned and my face must have said it all.
Jill asked.
  "What's wrong Peter?"… "You look as if you have just seen a ghost; I hope it's not bad news?"
I told them what Mr Sami said.
Jill immediately left her chair and gave me a hug and a kiss then calmly said.
  "We still got each other, even if I have to move into a caravan or a tent I will still love and care for you" … "Don't worry, we will work it out; and always remember our vows; "For better or for worst" … "You and I have both been through the worst; and for "Richer or poorer" … "We were rich and now poorer" … "Also, till death which I hope will not happen for a very long time to come before we part."
That answer proved to me that my wife was a priceless jewel in my life.

I telephoned my bank manager the next morning from my home office; he was a close friend and always called me Peter and I called him John, until I told him the news which he was already aware of from a memo he and all managers had received from head office about the collapse of the financial system in that particular country.

John replied with an official tone in his voice and said.

"Can you leave his matter with me Mr Gee; I will have to get advice from my head office to see if I can buy you and your accountant extra time to find a solution to your problem"

"Why are you addressing me as Mr. Gee, John?"

"Sorry I have to be professional with such a serious situation on my hands"

"Thank you, John"… "Or should I address you as SIR! from now on?"

He wasn't pleased with my answer and said.

"There is no need for sarcasm it just doesn't suit you"

I slammed the phone down, and after a four lettered slang word which I shouted out in temper; by the way it was a word with reference to a woman's private parts; my eyes began to fill with tears not because I stood to lose all, but the change in attitude from a man whom I thought was my friend and a regular visitor to my parties, my daughter's weddings, and the numerous past help I gave him to strengthen his position in the bank.

Afterwards the famous wise words entered my mind when Rose told me that it was harder when you come down the ladder.

I felt as if I was alone and stranded on an island until Jill came in from the kitchen and asked me if John has come up with a solution.

I replied and said that he didn't seem very worried and nor should she be anymore.

She wasn't convinced and passed me a cheque for £30,000.

I tore it up and told her not to be silly, the problem will solve itself in a few days.

That by the way was all the money she had in her savings which she accumulated over the years after my initial deposit of £500.

I decided to bypass John and telephoned his head office direct.

The manager there asked me how much my overdraft facility was and to save him time looking them up; I replied 5 million.

He then asked me how long I needed; I replied I can raise 4 million which would leave me with approximately £500,000, and I could also easily cover that sum by the sale of my assets and property.

"Look Mr. Gee, how about if I gave you three months?"

"Thank you I won't let you down"

"I am sure you are a man of your word, also please don't mistake me for Father Christmas because I have already looked at your case and I am sure we as a bank are not taking too greater a risk with you."

I put the phone down and felt a little more confident.

Jill was still listening and asked.

"Where will you get this colour of money from?"

I laughed and replied.

"God will provide"

She began to laugh with me and asked.

"Do you know his telephone number?"

"Yes, stay in here and sit opposite me and just listen"

I picked up the telephone to put Mr Sami in the picture. He said that he was very sorry that he had landed me in this situation but assured me that there was still hope. He told his wife who was related to a foreign royal family and she had agreed to transfer 5 million from her private account, only as a temporarily loan, and would expect it back when she asked for it, also she would give me reasonable time to settle it.

With uncontrollable joy, I replied.

"Thanks a million Mr Sami, please give your lovely and stunning wife a big hug and a kiss from Jill and I"

He began to laugh and replied.

"Surely you mean 5 million Peter?"

Within three hours there was an immediate transfer of 5 million from a Swiss bank account to mine, which was followed by a call from John who said.

"Good news Peter your account is now in credit after a direct and huge transfer from a reputable bank. Also, such transfers are only made at high management level" ... "How did you do it?"

I pretended to yawn and answered.

"It's who you know and not what you know. I would appreciate it if you address me as Mr Gee or Sir from now on" ... "I am a very busy man" ... "Is there anything else on your mind?"

Then with hurt I put the phone down on him.

Jill began to laugh and said.

"You are one cheeky bugger and that's why I love you" ... "So, now I know Mr Sami's wife is either God or the red-headed women you've been dating behind my back."

I put the staff on temporary half pay until I could sort things out with my accountant to begin calling my debts in.

Some of the staff left and I could understand why as they had families and commitments and could not manage on half pay.

The business picked up again but in no way as good as it was.

Mr Sami's wife managed to recover her loan when her husband received a promissory note which the African country issued for foreign debts and he carried on utilising it in the country instead of bringing in outside funds to pay the locals their wages and their own business expenses.

Neither Mr Sami nor I got away scot-free from our terrifying experience.

Shortly afterwards he suffered a stroke and nearly passed on, so he and his wife decided to come to England and underwent an emergency bypass operation which saved his life.

I, on the other hand, began to drink and smoke heavily and it affected my voice which was almost down to a whisper. Jill kept on at me and begged me to go and visit my GP to get it sorted out, but I told her not to worry too much and that I would promise to cut down on my smoking and drinking.

Harry was sitting at the breakfast table one morning and didn't look well.
I asked him.
   "What's up Harry?"
With a worried look on his face he replied.
   "Don't know son, I just don't feel right; I feel bloody lousy"
I knocked on my next-door neighbour who was a doctor and asked if he would please take a quick look at Harry.
He came in and pinched the back of Harry's hand and said.
   "This man is dehydrated and needs hospital attention."

Jill and I rushed Harry to our local hospital which was less than a five minutes' drive from our house and he was admitted.
After checks he was declared healthy and was discharged.
Jill and I decided to sell the house because it was getting too large for us especially with the girls moving out, we didn't need the extra rooms, also the bills were very high.

CHAPTER 15

We decided to stay in the area and bought a smaller house away from the main road. By then the eldest daughter married, followed by number two who married a labourer which we employed on one of our building works, and number three married the son of our baker whose shop was next door to the hairdressers where she worked.

When it came to number four, she met up with a young man who worked as a butcher's boy and ran errands for his father who owned the shop. They were the wealthiest of them all but extremely mean towards our daughter. If ever signs were written in the 'sand and stars' they were then, but regrettably we didn't take much notice of them.

We lived near a church, in a matter of fact only two doors away. The vicar became a good neighbour and friend. Jill and I often socialised together with him and his wife.

We decided to have number four's wedding ceremony in his church and the reception at our house afterwards. The catering was supervised by Jill's cousin, who still lived near us. The wedding and the marriage started to go wrong right from the start.

On the morning of the wedding Jill was getting her daughter, the bride, ready. Jill decided to put eye drops in her eyes to clear the tiredness from them. There was one almighty scream heard from the bedroom and we rushed upstairs to see what was wrong. Somehow Jill accidently put super glue in her eye as the bottle was very similar.

I put her in my car and told them to carry on with the wedding. Our daughter came out crying and was adamant that the wedding should be cancelled, and she would come with us, but Jill insisted that she carried on without her and wished her luck.

I managed to get Jill to the Accident and Emergency department quickly. Miraculously the doctor managed to save her eye. We returned to the church and my friend, the vicar, had decided to delay the ceremony until we had returned.

She got married and we still have proof of that unforgettable incident by the wedding photos showing Jill wearing her sunglasses in all the snaps and still smiling with defiance.

Two girls were still at home, well to be honest only one which was our baby as the other went to the Royal Masonic Boarding school in Rickmansworth, because I took out a policy with my bank for their education when the going was good.

History repeated itself and another bad deal left us with limited income, so we had no choice but to move again. Jill didn't mind, in a matter of fact she loved moving.

We went to see the local estate agent. When we met him neither of us could believe our own eyes because he and I were good friends from the City and worked for the same tea company, but lost contact, the last time I saw him was when our first daughter was born and he had come to our first house that had cost me £1,700 and the baby in his arms.

The market and the area by then was in great demand and the property shot up sky high, so he suggested that we bought his father's house.

When we got there, he introduced us to him and we got on like a house on fire, especially when I found out that he was ex-RAF, also a member of the dam-buster's squadron. We both had a lot to talk about and exchanged views. He was widowed and wanted to move into a home more for companionship than hardship or ill health. We snapped the house up at a reduced price because Jill fell madly in love with it and we moved.

Six months had past. Harry felt under the weather again and was admitted to the local hospital. He was in a coma for two weeks but never alone because Jill, her sister and the girls were by his bedside all the time. On Christmas day, 12.06 am, he sadly passed to join Rose, he was 84 years old.

Please remember this day and time, it's extremely significant to this biography.

By Harry passing away it didn't only leave Jill and I devastated with our girls but also her sister and connections.

My voice by then was almost down to a whisper. Jill almost frog-marched me to our local GP, short of a whip; he was also a friend and assured me that it was an allergy from the yellow rape which the local farmer was growing in the field opposite our house and not to worry too much about it.

It was a warm Friday evening, but I began to shiver and asked Jill to fetch me my coat and also to put the central heating on.
I almost cuddled the radiator but still felt very cold. Jill drove me to the surgery and insisted this time that he gave me a thorough examination.
His nurse came in and whispered to him.
His face drained from colour and then told me that I should go to Barnet General Hospital first thing in the morning.
He made an emergency appointment for me to see a specialist who was a colleague of his.
We returned home and went straight to bed.
Jill began to cry and cuddled me like a baby.
Her closeness and touch felt warm and comforting, just like the morning sun and made me feel safe in her arms, it also felt different from any other time, I just can't explain it.

She woke me up early in the morning and asked me how I felt.

I just shook my head negatively because I had no voice left.

We got into her car and during that short drive she kept telling me off like a mother would her naughty child.

There were tears pouring down her cheeks and in between her sobs and with loss of temper, she carried on saying.

"How many times have I told you to cut down on your bleedin' drinking and smoking" … "Specially your smoking, 80 fags a day" … "You stunk the house out" … "Just open your cupboard at home when or if we get back that is, and take a whiff, it will smell like an ashtray" … "Oh-no, you had to be a macho man" … "Now look at the mess you got us into" …. "Selfish that's what you are" … "Bloody selfish" … "I just don't know what I will do without you"

I kept pointing to the windscreen to tell her to keep her eyes on the road.

You know in reality she was taking advantage of me because I lost my voice; a form of loving bullying.

We arrived at reception and they directed us to the department. The specialist didn't turn up that day, but a young Chinese student doctor examined me and asked the nurse to immediately fetch another senior doctor. After the examination and with a serious tone in his voice he said and also drew Jill into the conversation.

"I am very sorry to say that you have a tumour in your Larynx, and we must drain it immediately, unfortunately being a Saturday we have no anaesthetic present here today and no time to transfer you to another hospital; if you agree I can give you an injection to numb the area and carry out the surgery."

Jill interrupted him and said.

"Well! What are you waiting for; get on with it."

They carried out the procedure and afterwards said that we could go home but to make sure that I kept the area clean and dry all the time then to return in five days, to see Mr Stern the head of the team.

It was a very trying period and Thursday took it's time to arrive.

Eventually on the Thursday we went to see Mr Stern and the only way to describe him was a "Gentle Man".

He told us that he must carry out a major operation, a total Laryngectomy; that is the removal of the Larynx or voice box, what we commonly call an Adam's apple, and then divert the airway from the nose and mouth to the bottom of the neck and breath through a stoma, also it will leave me without voice.

I had no other alternative because the cancer was at an advance and dangerous stage.

I was admitted, and the operation was carried out by one of Mr Stern's top students.

I felt a gentle tap on my face afterwards and a voice saying.
 "Please wake up Peter."

I opened my eyes and thought I was in heaven with a blue-eyed angel wearing a mask on her mouth and nose looking down on me; one of her warm tears fell on to my face. I smiled and thought that sight is better than heaven and all of its angels put together, it was my Jill.

I tried to tell her that I was okay but there was no sound coming from my mouth; yes, I was truly dumb.

I had to write everything down on paper afterwards when I wanted to converse, but trust me on this one, it was better than the alternative if I didn't agree to the operation.

Jill was not only my love, guardian angel and my dancing queen, but my strength to carry on with life although I felt handicapped.

It wasn't long after my radiotherapy, which was administered to me at Mount Vernon Hospital, I went back to Barnet General and underwent a further minor operation which was carried out by Mr Stern and had a prosthesis fitted in the stoma in my neck and got my voice back or let's say a voice very much similar to the natural one.

All this, without my Jill, I would not have made it. By the way that was 29 years ago so that proves that one can survive the mighty cancer with the following virtues of love, hope, good care, and perseverance.

CHAPTER 16

We moved out of Hadley Wood and bought a show house in Welwyn Garden City. Life in the 'Garden City' was trouble and hustle free and it was away from the mad, mad, busy business world.

Jill and I were sitting in the back garden one day; I honestly thought she loved gardening more than me; I was fascinated to see how the small shrubs which she planted had begun to grow into trees and the flowers had changed colour as one batch served its time and was replaced by another throughout the season.

It wasn't a huge garden, in a matter of fact very small compared with our Hadley Wood gardens, but if ever the 'Garden of Eden' was on this earth Jill made it more beautiful and colourful. This was another example of quality that counts and not quantity.

We were disturbed that day by Baby Emma who by then was grown up and as beautiful as her other five sisters. She introduced us to her latest boyfriend.
Have you ever had the experience that you have been there before, déjà vu, well that was unmistakable! I thought it just can't be young Kevin from Wellington Road, simply because his nose wasn't running?
Yes, I was right, and it was him.

They ended up getting married in Enfield registry office and we gave them the best reception we could afford in our home with their friends and close family and it was wonderful because it was friendly, intimate, personal and a private gathering.

Not long after, a few very happy years went past Jill and I began to enjoy a different dimension in our lives; the arrival of grandchildren.

We both adored them, and they adored us, but Jill had the edge over me because she spoiled them silly. They not only loved and idolised her but also enjoyed her food which was never rationed out to them when they visited us, and that was often.

Although we were extremely happy in Welwyn, we got itchy feet again, so Jill and I found a new built property in Goffs Oak and moved there. It started well, and on my birthday the girls and their husbands treated us to a long weekend break in New York.

Two weeks before we travelled Jill had to go into hospital for a minor operation and we could not cancel the booking. Rather than to disappoint me, also she knew that New York had always been my dream city to visit, she decided to brave it, although I told her that we could fly there another time when she felt better.

It was a dream come true and fulfilled for me, and we flew to Kennedy Airport. Although she felt poorly throughout the three days and camouflaged her discomfort and pain, she still never complained.
Sorry I deviated from the truth there, as she did complain when we visited the Italian sector.
Jill said.
"I don't like it here; everyone is Italian"
So, we walked to China Town, and then she said.
  "This is worse!"
I stopped her and completed the sentence by adding.
  "I don't like it here cos they are all Chinese?"
She laughed and replied.
  "You will never change and will always be Peter with a 'P'".
That's just another example why I loved her so much.

We returned to England and thanked the kids for the wonderful holiday.

Life with Jill continued to be fun. In a way we felt scared because we were so happy and contented in each other's company.

CHAPTER 17

The daughter who married the butcher's boy was unfortunately diagnosed with breast cancer, but prior to that she foolishly kept it to herself. When she no longer could stand her secret alone, she shared it with her mother. After she complained to Jill, she immediately took her to her GP.

She was in her late thirties at the time with four young children. She had a private mastectomy operation and recovered well. This was followed by chemotherapy treatment which stopped the cancer from spreading.

There was a lapse of three years and she even managed to get work by lifting heavy tables in the local tennis club to get extra pocket money for her children. After a while she was finding it difficult and her eldest son used to give her a hand with her work.

The cancer returned and she started chemotherapy again and lost her hair for the second time but still looked stunning.

One day whilst visiting us Jill took the children to our local supermarket to buy them sweets and left her with me. She began to cry and asked me through her sobs.
"Dad, am I going to die?"
I felt a lump in my throat and left to the toilet and broke down.
Afterwards I washed my face with cold water to freshen up; controlled myself and returned. She confronted me again and said.
"You didn't answer me, dad?"
I replied truthfully.
"I honestly don't know."
Before the conversation carried on, I was saved by Jill's return with the children who as soon as they entered the

room ran to their mother to show her what their nice nanny whom they adored had bought them.

The evil cancer which many have had the misfortune to know about is a cowardly disease and has no consideration and mercy towards its victims, it began to spread.
The legal department, acting for the private treatment insurance company, found a clause to stop further payments to the private hospital. No one came forward to fund it although many close members of the family could afford to.

Jill and I no longer had that sort of money to give towards the treatment which could have prolonged our daughter's life, even after we asked our bank to advance the funds against the deeds to our property, they declined.

So, the ever-faithful NHS stepped in and treated her, but it was too little and too late. She was discharged and sent home.

History once again was just about to repeat itself when arrangements behind my back were made to transfer her to a home which was four miles away.

All hell was let loose when Jill telephoned me and begged me to intervene because she was out numbered. I drove like a maniac to my daughter's house with one of my sons-in-laws who was married to number 5 and confronted them all.

A physical fight nearly broke out, and I was restrained by Sister Ann from the Convent who was visiting at the time because our daughter was forced to turn Catholic so that her children would be brought up in that faith.
I was told by one lady that my daughter would be in a better place and Sister Ann crossed herself.
I replied to the lady's remark and said.

"If she was your own daughter would you move her from her children and her own home?"
She replied.
"We are talking about your married daughter, also if we were to transport her back to the local hospital, she would never make it."
My temper flared up again and I shouted back.
"Would you please explain to me, because I am a little thick and not as clever as you; why in heaven's name can't she make the journey to the local hospital and the private ward which is five minutes away and yet you are going to send her to one of your homes four miles away in a congested traffic area?"... "Well!!... Answer me please?".
"I am sorry I don't have to discuss this issue with you anymore I will carry on and speak to her husband."
One of my daughter's closest member from their family and who was supposedly worth several millions said to me after lighting a cigarette.
"She has no quality of life"
I quickly stopped him and said.
"Every breath one takes is quality in life."
While all this argument was still going on neither her husband, or his mother interfered and just stood and watched.
I said to Jill.
"Would you object if we take our daughter back home where she belongs and put her up in our house?"
"There was no need to ask my permission we are still her parents!"
A carer nurse stepped in and said.
"We can bring a special bed for her here and keep a twenty-four hour watch over her."
Jill and I, and our girls, stepped in united. We said we would all take it in turns to be with her by her bedside all the time.

After several weeks our daughter lost her fight because the cancer spread like locust in her body and eventually affected her brain.

This was a devastating blow to us all. It caused a split in the family after two of our daughters sided together and the other three became united together with Jill and me. The feud is unfortunately still going on today after a decade.

Jill and I kept in touch with our grandchildren and used to take them out to the seaside which brought a smile on their faces and often took them home with us for regular meals which they missed and always loved.

Jill and I use to drive in our car to our daughter's house and collect them in their mother's seven-seater space waggon. However, the car was sold six months after our daughter had died by their other grandmother, who had by this time moved in with her son. This made it impossible for us to take the children out anymore and we woefully drifted apart.

Truly it was paradise lost and it happened so fast, just like an avalanche thundering down a snowy mountain, not only because of the grandchildren, but also the loss of our daughter and the drift between our daughters which was encouraged by outside influence.

You know our girls were once united, and inseparable with one motto; "All for one and one for all".
Don't get me wrong when they fought each other at home, it was often like world war three breaking out, but yet if an outsider was to harm one of them, they had to answer to the other five.

We still haven't seen one daughter and she has never made any attempts to visit us, yet the other did.

They say that absence makes the heart grow fonder, but in my opinion it doesn't; I believe out sight, out of mind, especially when the love is lost.

CHAPTER 18

We were now all getting on with our own lives that was Jill and I and our three girls with their children, our grandchildren. Some had been blessed with more children and given us a new title of 'great grandparents', a bonus which we enjoyed, but it's not a replacement because we still carried the pain for our lost daughter, which was also shared by all of her sisters.

You know one day I was in our local supermarket and a young girl, about 20 years old plus, came up to me and said.
  "You don't remember me, do you?"
I replied.
  "Should I?"
She said.
  "I am your granddaughter"
I simply replied.
  "Pleased to meet you" ... "Your grandmother is sitting in the car outside she would love to meet you again."
How sad is that!

Let's return to the more pleasant things in life.
One of our daughters, number 5, moved to Spain with her new husband because her first marriage had broken down. She landed on soft grounds because her new husband showed love and was treating her well.

Jill and I often went to visit them in Spain and sometimes met up with the other daughter together with her husband and children. Those were truly happy and intoxicating times.
Back home we carried on spending many happy times as a family, still present by the way, and often booked holidays together in the beautiful English green countryside. We stayed in cottages and farms with our three dogs, one German Alsatian and Cocker Spaniel which belonged to baby Emma and not forgetting our Charlie, the older brother to the Cocker Spaniel which Emma owned.

Yes, we seemed to have rekindled our happy days with nothing but laughter, BBQ's and the liquid which went with them to wash it down.

The loveliest of all people to meet at such gatherings were Kevin's parents and older brother who were our neighbours when we lived in Wellington Road.

CHAPTER 19

One day Jill told me that she had a water infection and I took her to the GP who prescribed pills for her and they seemed to work and cleared it. However, soon after she was beginning to get under the weather again and said to me one day.

"I still don't feel right?"

I replied.

"Right in the car and now. I am taking you to your GP and this time I will go in with you, also I promise not to give you an ear bashing like you gave me once"

She blushed and replied.

"No, you're not; it's a woman's problem; just take me there and wait in the car park. Also, you deserved the ear bashing you got from me that time."

They prescribed a stronger pill and that problem seemed to have been solved.

One day we were walking the dog in the field and Jill was struggling to keep up with me. I noticed that her stomach was getting bigger and it brought back memories to her old pregnancy days which made me laugh.

She asked me what was funny, and could she share my joke.

I said.

"Surely, you can't get pregnant when you are over 70 years old, or can you?"

She replied with a worried look on her face and said.

"You can be a very cruel bastard sometimes, but I am glad in a way you've noticed it"

"Look let's take the dog back home and we will go and see your GP and this time like it or not I am going in with you"

…. "By the way what are you going to name number 7"

I was trying to laugh it off, but it backed fire on me when she kept silent.

We returned home to drop the dog off. I telephoned the surgery and told them it's an emergency and we need to see a doctor immediately. The receptionist returned and said you are in luck and if we could come straight away and ask Jill to bring a water sample with her. Without any hesitation we left and headed to the surgery.

On our arrival Jill begged me not to go in with her because she felt embarrassed and to wait in the car. I told her that it will be okay, but she was to insist on a blood test this time. I sat in the car and it seemed ages before she came out with a piece of paper and said that we must go to the local hospital and get an urgent blood test.

The next day another doctor from the surgery telephoned and asked Jill if she could come immediately to the clinic as her blood tests results were back.
After her visit she came out looking devasted and was sobbing her heart out.
I asked her what was wrong.
She replied.
  "He said I have to go back now to the hospital to have a CA125 blood test"
  "What's that?"
  "He thinks I have ovarian cancer"
I shouted out aloud and tears began to roll down my face.
  "No, no, no, please God not that again"
The blood test was taken, and we returned home.

By 5'oclock that day the surgery telephoned us and asked if Jill could return. This time I went in with her and the doctor confirmed that Jill had ovarian cancer and her CA125 blood test unfortunately indicated a very high count which meant that it was at an advanced stage 4.
I lost my temper and said to him.
  "Why in heavens name did you let it go to an advanced stage, she has been given pills for a water infection for the last six months?"
  "I sympathise with you Mr. Gee, but it is sometimes very difficult to detect this type of cancer"

"Don't sympathise with me doctor, it's Jill who you should be feeling sorry for! The most important thing is; what are you going to do about it?"

"She will receive the very best medical treatment on offer." … "Although it is at an advanced stage it's not terminal yet, and every day new treatments are being discovered, also we hope to find it soon."

Jill was sent to the local hospital to have the water in her stomach reduced and was discharged two days later feeling extremely comfortable with the reduced size of her tummy.

She and I knew that we had a long and agonising journey ahead of us that had been learned that from our past experience. We also knew that we were both fighters and would persevere with whatever was thrown at us, only because we had a head start which was our strong and unmeasurable love for one another, also the love from the rest of the family. However, most of all we had FAITH AND HOPE.

CHAPTER 20

We were sent to another local hospital to access the growth of the cancer. The results showed that the tumours had not spread and the specialist there was by sheer luck a member of a team which practiced at the UCL Hospital in Euston Road, a newly built hospital from the previous one which we unfortunately had to visit for the termination when Jill's mother had her problems, but this time it was for her salvation.

Jill was chosen for a trial which was very limited nationwide. Her treatment commenced with an operation to remove some of the tumours, but this was stopped short because of complications. However, it was followed by a course of a new chemotherapy. Amazingly the CA125 blood test count began to go down; that was a good sign because it indicated that the treatment was working, and the tumours were shrinking, the most important thing of all the results were a booster to us, we sharpened our sabres and went into battle against the cancer again.

Jill had one of the nicest oncologists anyone could ever wish for. She was friendly, kind and sympathetic. Like many, she loved Jill and we all equally loved her dearly and treated her as one of the family. Credit must also be given to every single member of that hospital, from the cleaner to the top surgeon, because they all were a good team, a machine which operated by love, affection and care to their patients.

A year past and Jill was doing well, her hair grew back again. She had asked for a wig and got one without any delay. On warm days she found the wig uncomfortable, so I told her, but failed to convince her, that she looked extremely sexy without one.

She replied by saying.

"We'll do a deal; you shave your hair off and I will stay sexy without a wig only for you."

She then began to laugh only because she knew I was still conceited.

We decided to book a farm in Dorset for two weeks and the other girls turned up and stayed for a couple of days. It was a memorable holiday and far away from the maddening crowed, because Thomas Hardy, the author of that book, used to live across the road to the farm and we visited his house which was open for public viewing.

Jill returned to chemo' and miraculously she continued to improve. She became tired from the treatment and asked her oncologist if she could have a break. She advised her to persevere as breaking the treatment at that stage would be to her disadvantage. But Jill could not carry on and asked members of the family for their advice. The girls and I told her to persevere, but she decided to stop the treatment and go on tablets instead. It was easier for us to say persevere because we didn't feel her discomfort.

That was a set back because her CA125 blood test indicated that the cancer was on the move again. So, her oncologist put her on a different new drug from America but unfortunately it was too strong for her to handle. Rather than to stop it she decided to put Jill on a lower dose, but still she could not handle the discomfort and gave her a break.

Her oncologist still did not give up on her and put her back on the original chemo, but the damage was already done. Jill then began to fight back and was half way there but became too weak to handle the treatment. She became less mobile but still braved her shopping trips with the help of the trolley and spent most of her time laying on the settee watching the TV and listening to the 50's and 60's music with me.

I, with the girls, took over the housework and cooking and left her to rest. It was time for us to pay her back for the past years she slaved on us.

She didn't eat much by this stage and every day I looked at her and witnessed her determination to survive. She was still trying to cheer me up because she knew I was being tortured.

You know we still had fun even then. My daughter with her husband decided to move a double bed from one of the bedrooms into our small dining room as Jill just could not climb the stairs anymore. I could never figure out why every time I tried to help her by pushing her leg and placed it on the next step, she would not accept it, and slap my hand then insisted on doing it herself.

She would persevere and reach the last step but get a mental blockage and stop.

One day she really tried but failed halfway and I struggled to get her to the top.

By the time when we reached the landing, I had no more strength left, bearing in mind I was 80 years of age.

So, she collapsed on the floor and I fell next to her.

We looked at each other because neither of us could stand up and we burst out laughing.

She said.

  "We can't stay here all night; what are you going to do about it Mr know it all?"

Lucky for both of us I had the phone in my pocket and telephone Baby Emma.

She came down because she lived up the road and had a key to let herself in.

We looked at her shocked face when she saw us on the floor and all three of us burst out laughing.

She managed to get me up first and then we helped Jill into bed.

By the way that was the reason for moving the bed down to the dining room!

The first night I jumped into bed next to her from the bottom of the bed because there was no room on the sides, and I said.

"Does this bring back happy memories from 60 years ago?"

She with laughter replied.

"Do you know Peter I was also just thinking about that" … "Haven't you and I travelled a long way in our marriage; I wish we could go back to that room and start all over again."

"We could only reminisce and it's a shame we have to go only forward now"

There were other incidents which I repeatedly fell for; she used to wake me up, lick her lips, and say.

"You slept well; I am dying for a cup of tea and a boiled egg"

"What time is it?"

She would pretend to look at her wrist watch and reply.

"Half past seven"

I used to get out of bed and go to the kitchen then look at the clock on the wall and shout back"

"You lying cow Jill; it's only three o'clock"

Then, I would hear her in hysterical laughter ending with her famous words.

"Oh, don't I am going to wet myself."

Although cancer was winning the battle, I still had to put up a fight for my loved one.

I was beginning to get physically, mentally and emotionally weaker and pulled my back several times lifting her in and out of bed; I used to tell her to put her arms around my neck and then pulled her up slowly and afterwards placed my hands around her and held her close till we shuffled and reached the loo.

With tears and laughter, she joked and said. "Shall we jive or do the creep?"

She and I, during that trying time, shed rivers of tears between us discreetly and at the same time we avoided to show or share our pain and sorrow with one another, only our laughter did we have time for as we carried on with our battle against the degrading cancer.

CHAPTER 21

Jill's hope and positiveness was beginning to get weaker because she often used to reach a point of; "I've had enough" but not I. Jill was 77 years young and I do mean young, but unfortunately very sick.

She also knew I would never give up on her and would fight and destroy whatever or anyone who tried to harm her, our girls, or their children. That's why she bravely carried on with her battle and fought with me.

We were reaching the last stand against the demon and cowardly evil disease which was stealing my wife away from me and all those who loved and adored her.

She no longer could control her motions which left her with extreme embarrassment because she was still a shy, dignified and very private person; the thieving cancer also knew it but still showed no mercy on her.

I used to pray every day, night or whenever I had a spare moment but eventually my anger made me feel disillusioned with my faith and I simply gave up praying but never gave up hope and my fight for my soul mate Jill, I also thought that my God must have been deaf and did not seem to have his hearing aid on.

I knew that this wasn't God's will and in my own opinion the human race brought this upon itself by trying to equal their knowledge to him who was their creator, even after Adam and Eve's original sin we still have not learned our lesson. Mind you we are still in a better position to many less-advanced countries.

A commode was brought in by one of the NHS carers and placed near the bed. This made my life easier because I didn't have to take the long journey, or it seemed long to the hallway loo, but it didn't help Jill because she could not sit up or get out of bed on her own.

Adding more embarrassment and misery she had to have a change of disposable underwear several times in the night and I had to do it. When she objected, I reminded her that her memory was failing because I used to help her out with our girls when they were babies and she answered with a flushed face and said.

"I am 77 years old and not a baby anymore; Tut.Tut.Tut and I am losing it?"

Her legs began to swell, and she asked me to rub them. This helped to relieve the pain but not the swelling, so I told one of the carers about it and she brought a cream and told me how to rub her legs without causing Jill any further pain or discomfort.

Several weeks passed and Christmas was only 8 days away. I began to notice that Jill developed a phobia and did not want to stay in the dark, so one of the girls bought her a side lamp and we kept it on throughout the night. I often used to wake up after sensing that she was awake and notice that she was staring ahead of her.

One night I asked her.

"What's wrong?"

A tear left her eye and she replied.

"I know I am going to die and very soon."

I held back my own tears and tried to dismiss what she had just said and replied.

"Don't be bloody silly, go to sleep."

Then I placed my arm under her neck and kissed her.

She simply replied.

"Thank you; I needed that badly".... "You will always be MY hero" ... "Also, thank you for picking me instead of my friend Val" ... "What worries more than me dying is how will you mange without me?"

I replied.

"Thank you for forcing me to choose you and most of all thank you for being you and not Val."

She began to laugh and replied.

"Your mother was right when she referred to you as a clown; why can't you be serious for just one moment in your life?"

"We don't have much time to be serious Jill; besides its boring."

I caught her eyes in the light's reflection and was saddened because they seemed to have change in colour from the azure lively blue to tired grey eyes.

She noticed me looking and stroked my forehead first then my face.

Her touch felt different and not in a bad way because it felt so tender and loving as if she was passing a message onto me, but I never realised at the time, or did I and was blanking the truth out?

The next morning, I felt her staring at me but again I didn't ask her what was bothering her because I somehow knew and saw the fear on her face.

Christmas Eve finally arrived, and we all agreed that she will have the best Christmas ever. We would open our presents at her bedside and breakfast was to be held around her bed. Then in the afternoon we would have a simple buffet instead of roast turkey.

About 10'oclock that morning Jill complained of cramping pains at the top her stomach. I gave her two table spoons of Gaviscon, which made her burp, she apologised afterwards, then said.

"That's much better"

Opportunity knocked; I laughed and replied.

"Now, if that was me burping, I would have got a mouthful from you"

She looked at Emma, who was with us, laughed and said.

"As it's Christmas tomorrow I promise I will let you burp, but somehow I don't think I will be witnessing it."

The pain returned, this time it was unbearable for her; she asked Emma to drive her to the UCL Hospital in Warren Street. Emma instead telephoned the hospital for advice and they said that the journey may not do her any good for her, also she would have to wait for several hours in Accident and Emergency being Christmas Eve. They suggested she rang her GP for advice, but she could not get in touch with them because the surgery was closed.

We had no other option but to ring for an ambulance and they responded quite quickly.
Two medics, a man and a woman came into the house and they gave Jill a thorough examination. The lady medic administered a morphine injection to her. The male medic asked Jill if the pain was still there and she told him that it has eased off a little bit.

He wasn't happy with the situation and told Jill that he preferred her to agree if she would allow him to take her to the local hospital for a second opinion but could not take her to Warren Street because it was out of his area. She agreed; Emma and I accompanied her in the ambulance which took her to Barnet General.

On the way Jill kept begging us not to leave her there on her own. I assured her that we will be super glued to her until she returns back home with us.

I felt dazed and my thinking brain, what was left of it, could not function properly anymore. It was worse than a nightmare because I knew I was still awake, but I could not stop or do anything to change what was happening around me. Somehow and deep inside, I was trying to blank the truth out.

We arrived to the hospital and after a short wait Jill was pushed in on her stretcher, and as we promised, we held her hands on either side.

After that Jill was wheeled to a bed in a cubicle and they drew the curtains on us for privacy. Several doctors and nurses came in and out to examine Jill.

In the meantime, daughter number 3 arrived at the hospital with her husband and we all kept a visual. We hardly spoke to one another because we shared the same fear and yet Jill seemed to have cheered up and asked me to raise the pillow because she felt uncomfortable.

A nurse came in and attempted to remove her wedding ring beause her finger swelled up. After several attempts I told her to cut the ring off, but the nurse persevered and took out of her pocket a piece of string, then tied it behind the ring and managed to remove it; after that Jill stared down at her bare finger and smiled with tears rolling down her face.

She asked to be lowered and attempted to sleep. Her eyes began to roll; every time they closed, she shook her head to wake up and asked what the time was. This went on for two hours, or there about, and then she continually asked what the time was as if she was waiting for an urgent meeting and did not want to be late.

She managed to sleep for a few minutes and woke up startled by the noise from the other side of the curtains as the nurses, doctors and staff where beginning to celebrate with loud carol music playing in the back ground.
It was Christmas eve after all.
Jill looked at me and I was very familiar with that look because I knew that she was ready to tell me off or lecture me.
I wasn't wrong this time as always; she raised her voice and said.
  "Peter I can't take you anywhere without you showing me up" … "Turn that bloody music down and now!"
I began to laugh and the others including Jill joined me when I replied with a high pitched voice and said.

"It's not me Jill; honest it's the nurses outside."
She realised her error and apologised.

I asked her how she felt and if she still had pain, she replied that she felt well and was ready to go back home. Also, the first thing she fancied when she got there was a nice large glass of cold dry white wine.

We were interrupted by a nurse who came in carrying a tray with medication on it. I asked her what they were for and she told me that they are to ease the pain and vomiting.
I asked Jill.

   "Do you have any pain or feel sick?"
She smiled and answered.

   "No, I feel fine; no pain and even your face is not making me feel sick anymore"
Her answer brought laughter to the others.

The nurse carried on and injected her in her left side and left.
We carried on talking and joking with Jill who was on top form, considering. We were interrupted by the nurse again who injected Jill on her right side and then gave her a further injection in the arm on the left. Jill's eyes began to roll again, and she dosed off also seemed in a peaceful and comfortable sleep.

She woke up startled and stared in front of her as if someone was there and said.

   "Lift me up" … "Don't just stand there lift me up!"
I asked her who she was talking to?
And she replied.

   "Sorry I was only dreaming"
Her eyes began to roll again and then she vomited blood and said.

   "Oh, that's much better it must have been the coffee I had earlier."
We all knew that it wasn't coffee.
One of the girls went and fetched a nurse to clean her up.

Afterwards the nurse suggested to all of us if we would prefer to be in a more private and quieter room and we agreed. I wasn't happy with what was going on, so I left the cubicle and asked one of the nurses if I could see the doctor in charge.

He looked hassled and exhausted.

I asked him.

"What's going on with my wife?"

He asked who my wife was and then casually replied after looking at his paper work in his hand.

"Oh, yes she is dying"

I replied in a state of shock and said.

"What! And what are you doing about it?"

"There isn't much we can do" … "Because we all begin to die from the minute, we take our first breath"

"I am neither interested or concerned about all that; I am only interested in my wife right now and not your philosophy."

He cut me short and said.

"There are many other patients in the same state as your wife; if you would please excuse me sir, I am very busy because we are short on staff."

I returned to the cubical and held Jill's hand. After sixty years of marriage neither of us could hide our feeling from one another, and as soon as Jill saw me, she somehow knew that I was struggling with the situation; she gently nodded her head, then beckoned me over, smiled and whispered so that the others didn't hear her and said.

"I love you very much; I am sorry I couldn't express my true feelings to you, please be brave and strong as you have always been to me because our girls need a pillar to lean on."

I whispered back.

"Don't be bloody daft, you are the pillar, and we all still need you, also that in my opinion is a very good example of negative thinking"

"You will never change but please always stay as you are."

I left the cubicle because I could no longer hold back my aching pain and felt as if my heart was tearing. Emma joined me and went to see another passing doctor and insisted that he took a look at her mother. He asked a nurse for her notes and went into the cubicle then stood looking confused and then he simply replied.

"Sorry, this doesn't help you, but I am unable to comment simply because I am not familiar with this lady's case, if you will now please excuse me."

I stopped him and said.

"Why don't you say it" … "Because we are short of staff and its Christmas Eve!"

Then I shook my head helplessly.

He wasn't amused and left.

The nurse returned and wheeled Jill towards the private room.

Jill said to her on the way.

"Could you do me a big favour nurse instead of waiting for the ambulance would you leave me on this trolley and wheel me back home my husband Peter will show you the way."

The nurse laughed and replied.

"I can assure you Jill the ambulance will turn up."

We arrived at the private room and as soon as we entered one could only hear the sound of silence hissing in your ears.

THE FINAL HOUR

Jill went off to sleep and I sat on one side of the bed and held her hand and just stared at her. Her aged face became calmer and amazingly   younger. She was disturbed by the nurse who woke her up and gave her a further injection in the arm.

Jill looked at each one of us in turn, smiled and then dosed off again.
She repeated the same request that she had in the cubicle and asked us to lift her up.
Emma and I franticly turned a handle to raise her head.
She looked at us in turn and burst out laughing then said.
  "I wasn't talking to you two."

She then stared in front of her in the same way which by now we were very familiar with.
All of a sudden, we all felt a cold breeze enter the room, even the screen round the bed moved and yet no doors were opened.
Jill carried on saying and was still in laughter.
  "Whatcha, Mum, Dad, and you Mandy and just look at you nan you look so lovely".... "Please lift me up they are all driving me mad down here because they think I am talking to them."
The room became warm again and she closed her eyes and smiled.
Then she opened them again and they began to roll also she was trying hard to stop them by continuously shaking her head.
For that short moment I noticed that her eyes turned azure blue again and sparkled; her face became free from wrinkles and she looked as if she was 17 again.

She went into a deep sleep and we could hear her breathing loudly, then opened her eyes again smiled and whispered.
  "Bye my darlings"
Emma looked at me and I nodded my head.

It was Christmas day, 12:06 am, and that was the end of "My Dancing Queen" on this planet. I knew that she would never suffer any earthly pain again and also, she "WILL" be happy and looked after in her eternal and spiritual life.

A NOTE TO THE READER

This is Jill's story and it does not apply to all who are fighting the cancer she had.

Also, the treatment and the trials which they carried out on Jill, and many others, are paving the way closer to finding a cure for cancer.

Doctors and patients alike are brave soldiers and taking risks and sacrifices to make our future world free from genetic, and many other diseases.

The sacrifice, pain and heartache will never go unrewarded nor will it be forgotten by all those connected in this united front to fight this curse on the human race.

Printed in Great Britain
by Amazon